Robin

The Sea, Jimmy Beerkeg and Me

COPYRIGHT

Copyright © 2020 Robin Sheldon Kenny All rights reserved.

No part of this book may be reproduced, or stored in a retrieval system, or transmitted in any form or by any means, electronic, mechanical, photocopying, recording, or otherwise, without express written permission of the publisher.

ISBN-13: 9798683722159
ISBN-10: 1477123456

Cover design by: Ruth Hickson.

Cover picture reproduced with the kind permission of Alex Kafka.

Library of Congress Control Number: 2018675309

Printed in the United Kingdom

For my brilliant boys

Joshua and Dominic.

INTRO

"Torpedoes, Skip"

You never seem to get any real sleep on a boat at sea no matter how long the voyage lasts or how knackered you are. You slumber in fits and turns in a dreamlike state somewhere between consciousness and the great Land of Nod with the constant background sounds of the sea: waves slapping the hull inches from your head; grinding winches; flapping sails; massively noisy diesel engines going on and then off again before occasional jaw-dropping words penetrate the consciousness; words like 'torpedoes', for instance. I opened my eyes. A dark shadow, stolid and unmoving loomed, hovering above my bunk. A thin red night light from the saloon scattered recognition as my drowsy sleep-dulled mind sharpened and resolved itself into something approaching reason. The face of Jimmy Beerkeg stared down at me.

A man apparently untroubled by emotions Jimmy had decided, for his own private reasons, to adopt me years ago as a sailing companion and had taken on a doggedly faithful and oddly protective manner ever since. Nowadays Jimmy always referred to me as 'Skip' or occasionally when he was really trying to impress 'Skipper'. In my dulled state of mind, I wondered briefly if he actually knew my real name.

Trying to sleep is one thing, but actually waking up on a vessel at sea, particularly a little one out in a big ocean, can also be more than a tad disconcerting. The first drowsy seconds tend to go something like this:

"Where the hell am I?" You're on a sailing boat.

"Why are we moving – we're in harbour!?" We're moving because we're at sea.

"Where are we?" Atlantic, North.

"The wind's picked up!" Not really, seems the same to me.

"Why are we going the wrong way?" We're not you're just confused because you're still half asleep. You went off watch 2 hours ago and have endured broken sleep ever since, waking

every 10 to 15 minutes. We have one reef in the main and one reef in the jib. Well, at least we did when you were last up.
"Did he just say torpedoes?" eh yes, I think he did.

"Torpedoes, Jimmy? You're saying someone is firing at us!?" I exclaimed rubbing my eyes and stalling for time.
"Off the starboard bow, first one missed I reckon" continued Jimmy in his relentless way. Not for the first time I tried to pin the accent down, Northern definitely (to a soft Southerner like me anyway) but was it Derbyshire? Yorkshire? Lancashire? I dragged myself out of my pit.
"Torpedoes." I said again, pointlessly. I felt my instinctive bile rising. Annoyed that I had been woken and at the same time aware that standing orders are 'always wake me if you're worried about anything, anything at all including hostile military aggression'. Never get angry with crew when they're simply following your orders. The rest of the time is just fine, however.

I stumbled up onto deck. Pitch black. No moon now and plenty of cloud cover. Helm ticking away under autopilot. I'm conscious I need to get my night vision sorted but know that will take precious minutes. I sensed Jimmy's large bulk moving slowly up the companion way stairs behind me. I looked at him again. Big bushy beard. Indeterminate age, around 60 something?

Maybe older? He was dressed for the night watch; jacket, sailing trousers, hat, head torch with his life jacket and harness on. I was in boxer shorts.

"Another one coming Skip!" shouted Jimmy looking off to starboard, pointing midships approximately 30 foot off. I looked and saw what he meant. Straight-line, an object moving at high speed illuminated by millions of microscopic creatures, the bioluminescence exploding into countless individual tracers as the missile shaped horror moved swiftly upon its deadly trajectory straight for the centre of our vessel. I stumbled back for an instant in horror. It was one of those scenes from a black and white World War II film come suddenly to life. My God.

Then I finally woke up. And laughed. Delighted to see once again one of the most joyful sights that a yacht delivery skipper is confronted with during those long, long, lonely night watches. The mysterious object, now just 10 feet off our beam veered suddenly forward, turning, wraithlike to its right, a ghost of the sea, about 6 feet in length and going like the clappers, mocking our own swift progress through the seas. Shooting past the bow it turned and dived down under the anchor, spun on a crest and surfed our bow wave with quick little bursts of bioluminescent fireworks crackling behind it. A common dolphin, invisible itself in this moonless night, now illuminated in glorious sparkling profile as it dived and soared. A crystal robed Prince glorying for a moment in his own salty kingdom, the mighty sea.

I smiled and shook my head.

"Bioluminescence, Jimmy. It's just a common dolphin playing at the bow".

Jimmy stood silently, faced forward, with his usual inscrutable regard, legs slightly apart holding his impressive bulk steadily and lightly as the vessel swayed gently to and fro. We stood together in the cockpit in companionable silence observing one of the many wonderful sights provided free of charge in this world's deep oceans.

"Fuckin' dolphins" he said.

YACHT DELIVERY SKIPPER

"You do WHAT for a living?".

A village event. A mate's 40th. There is music playing quite loudly but we can just about make ourselves heard. A local Dad holding a half-finished pint is looking incredulously at me. He is frowning. He leans closer. I can smell his breath now. I try not to look at him whilst I respond in a neutral voice:
"I sail small to medium sized sailing boats from A to B. The agency I work with deals with the owner, provides crew, books my flights, sends me the necessary charts and pilots books and so we just, normally at least, rock up at the airport, you know, Gatwick, Heathrow, whatever" I shrug, "fly out to the boat

wherever that happens to be" I shrug again," Caribbean, Mediterranean, North America, Hawaii, Cape Town, whatever and then we sort the boat out, run through some pre-checks" (I'm sounding like an automaton again) "then we sail to wherever the boat needs to be (UK, Greece, Turkey, Sweden wherever) clean it up, go out and have a beer or two and then, when everything is sorted we fly home again. Job done".

"And you actually get paid for this?"

"Yeh...not much though", I add weakly.

Then comes the summary.

"You get PAID to sail around the Caribbean in someone else's luxury boat."

I smirk although I don't mean to.

"So, these boats then? They're worth millions aren't they?"

"Some are worth millions absolutely, but others much less, owners tend to be quite rich of course" My companion raises his eyebrows and looks amused. I continue on hastily "but not mega rich, these aren't super yachts with dodgy Russian billionaire owners, they're around 40 to 60 feet typically and most of the owners are really decent, hard-working guys who are perhaps cash rich but time poor so I get their boat to where they want it to be and then they can fly out there and sail the area whatever that may be…. like the Caribbean Sea or coast of Norway or back here on the South Coast for instance".

It's normally at this stage of the conversation that my curious companion standing next to me becomes rather animated and begins to employ colourful language (if the event is child-free that is). I reassure them that although the job does sound like one big holiday with me and some blokes having a whale of a time sailing the high seas and drinking ourselves to death at every port, the more I try to describe the 'dangers of the deep', 'the accidents', 'risks', the remarkable levels of discomfort, and the moments of true terror, the more he laughs and claps me on the back and tells me what a lucky bastard I am. He then goes on to tell me what he does for a living and assures me that it never involves flitting around beautiful island chains with female crew ("You get girls onboard too?!" His eyes bulging. "Well, yes sometimes crew are female, yes" I stutter) and he then goes on to tell me that he works in I.T. and sometimes he gets out of the office to visit Swindon ("SUNNY Swindon", he says with emphasis) and once he had to go to a conference in Staines ("That's STAINES", he says his eyes revolving in his sockets).

The next step is also inevitable.

"Oii, Darren (or whomever), you should hear what this bloke does for a living!"

Signalling his mates behind him, they stagger into the conversation. Several pints have now been consumed, the conversation is genial and free flowing. The music is ramping up. Darren staggers overs, listens to his mate and frowns, gets closer and bellows above the music:

"You do WHAT for a living?"

And so it goes on.

Not that I'm complaining of course. I'd spent many years myself in offices; wandering aimlessly around the endless corridors and back door warrens of the British Museum pretending to work and then, driven by an insane impulse to actually make some money, had a go at being a young upwardly mobile manager for a 'leading blue chip company in the City' as the blurb went. Trips to New York, dining out in posh restaurants pretending we were paying with our own money, wearing important business suits with real silk ties and looking serious for a living I was pretty content for a while. Well, until they laid me and everybody else off anyway.

Armed with a surprisingly generous golden handshake (such was their eagerness to get shot of me) unattached, 35 years of age and having managed to insinuate myself on to the property ladder, I was free to take on new and exciting challenges. So, I decided to look for another office job but this time with more money. In the meantime, however, before I took my pick of senior important office roles that would no doubt come flooding through my door I would sign up for a 4 month sailing course on the South Coast with one of the most prestigious sailing schools in the land. I'd blow it all and go to sea. Well, for 4 months anyway. Then I'd get a real job again.

That was many years ago now.

ASTRID

"SAIL THE CARIBBEAN SEA ON A SQUARE-RIGGED SAILING VESSEL! TRAINEES NEEDED FOR THE ADVENTURE OF A LIFETIME!"

My interest in water had started with paper 10 years before. Not any old paper but the Sunday Times. One morning found me scanning through my Dad's copy and I spotted the above advert. The closest I'd got to adventure on the high seas was being violently and rather dramatically sick on HMS Belfast when I was about 5. None of my multitude of siblings had ever been near a boat apart from one brother who'd decided to take a local Scout troop's small sailing boat on its trailer down to the local lake with his mates only to discover that in order to get the sails up you needed something called a 'boom' which had inadvertently been left back at the hut many, many miles away. No doubt they made valiant efforts but were doomed to flap meaninglessly around the lake before giving up and going home. Much like real sailing in fact but they weren't to appreciate that at the time.

Anyway the advert obviously piqued my fancy and I found myself down in Weymouth in late Winter for a 'Selection Weekend'. I was 25 and thought myself a well-travelled and experienced young man ready for adventure and up for any challenges fortune could throw at me. I had yet to realise a 'Selection Weekend' was actually a 'do you have enough money to pay the large amounts required for you to support a square rigger for 3 months, if you do, you're in weekend'. The Astrid Sailing Trust had employed some crazy ex-army types to send us scurrying off into the night armed with a map, a list of mandatory check points and were generous enough to give us a compass too. Having built rope bridges, traversed raging rivers (well, it felt like they were raging) and orienteered our way to some obscure pub in the hills above Weymouth we were happily reunited with our trainers who spent the evening desperately impressing us with their fearsome adventures on land. Having regaled us with their army-fuelled anecdotes whilst getting us trainees to be 'mighty merry' on the local brew they then happily sent us off into the night with a NEW list of check points to keep us staggering around like lost sheep into the small wee hours of the night. Drunk, disorientated and half dead from fatigue the final 'test' upon arrival at the last check point on the list was to make our own shelter for the rest of the night out of some poles and leaves whilst our SAS / SBS / DHS special forces trainers skipped off to the local B & B for a decent night's kip.

At the final interview that afternoon (remember we hadn't finished blundering around in the dark until that morning) I realised the entire operation revolved around whether we could afford the enormous payment for the trip. If you could, you're in. The 28-year-old girl who had gamely struggled around the course with us and had been encouraged to join in despite the stated 18-25 age range sadly failed the selection process…. she was too old they said.

The tall ship Astrid was a 140ft two masted brig with the full set of big manly square sails on its 2 masts and 4 of those triangular ones that stick out on the bowsprit called jibs. She also, I discovered had another big sail at the stern on its own boom called rather oddly 'the Spanker'. I never did find out why. She had about 180 different lines all with different purposes and all made of the same cream coloured skin flaking sisal – to us trainees they all looked the same and apparently had something to do with raising the yards themselves or the square sails in between or something like that. God, I hate sailing books. It's all baggy wrinkling, handy billies and Bob's your Uncle. But we had to get our heads round it all because we'd met the Captain. And we'd all concluded in short order that the Captain was not a very nice man. Not a nice man at all.

Captain Frank Scott was an ex-Navy officer in his mid-fifties whose early retirement had thrown him, no doubt struggling and screaming, into the financial requirements of securing a couple more years of income. That income had come in the hesitant shape of 26 eighteen to twenty-five years olds most of whom had the parental income to afford the multiple thousands required to join Frank on Astrid. The fact that most of the young people on board came from well-to-do households was one of the many reasons why Frank hated us. Frank hated me because, at that stage of my life, I was thinking of going into banking. The Royal Bank of Scotland were actually toying with accepting me on to their graduate 'fast track' scheme, and so I was therefore a living embodiment of all of Frank's financial angst even though I had yet to step through the door of any RBS branch. Others incurred Frank's wrath for being young, female and competent or all these things together, which was even worse. He hated us with the passion of the truly sincere and took every opportunity to belittle and demean us as is the Great Tradition of the Sea. He would roam the decks with a fixed sneer on his twisted face and confront each hapless trainee attempting to look busy coiling lines or scrubbing decks with a uniquely crafted insult:

"Typical Welshman", Frank would sneer if you had a Welsh Aunt.

"Typical Dane", he'd say if you'd been to Denmark once.

"Typical... Trainee", if he had no idea who the hell you were but since you were onboard and under 25, a safe bet. I was a 'typical banker' of course. Frank, in other words, was a proper job Captain.

He was also highly experienced and very, very competent. Frank's primary job, he knew, was to survive the next 3 months in order to secure sufficient income to never have to sully his hands with 'trainees' ever again. But in order to achieve this goal he had to stay alive. There was a problem however, since on this, as on all other sail training ships that offer 'adventures of a lifetime' you have to, at some time or other, and however reluctantly, allow the trainees to actually touch things, pull things, climb things and steer things. This is a problem because the trainees are new to the ship, don't know how it works and could, if given sufficient scope, happily murder everyone on board. Which brings us to a general truism about sailing of which most of the general public are happily ignorant: sailing little boats in big oceans or indeed anywhere near hard bone-crushing land is not a safe and fun pursuit at all – it is actually eye-poppingly dangerous. When you fill a 140ft square rigged sailing vessel with 26 testosterone pumped young people who are entirely unaware of the various ways things can go horribly wrong, then you are elevating those risks to titanic levels. Frank, being the sensible experienced officer he was, knew this. We didn't.

On top of this, the voyage was an unusually ambitious one. Three months and over 5000 nautical miles starting from St. George's in the Windward Isles we would spend the first month sailing up through the numerous islands of the Caribbean chain towards the British Virgin Islands stopping en route to dive (another opportunity for disaster to occur, so Frank had this farmed out and therefore legally disowned all responsibility to a fresh faced twenty six years old dive instructor) before the first long ocean passage, 750 miles from the Virgin Islands up to Bermuda.

Having successfully blundered our way through both the Leeward and Windward islands we arrived, 40 days later, miraculously unscathed and, to everyone's surprise, just a couple of miles off Bermuda. Frank then had to endure the quiet agony of watching us trainees happily navigate through some of Bermuda's quite terrifying reefs (Bermuda's reef system is bigger than Bermuda itself) before we pulled into the old Royal Naval Docks in the island's northwest corner. Given several days off, we happily rented out 26 scooters and proceeded to charge around the island defying the local traffic to finish off what the Atlantic had so far failed to do.

Having briefly discharged all responsibility for us, Frank no doubt then turned his attention to the next big risk to his finances, the long haul across the Atlantic Ocean to Cork in southern Ireland. The distance from Bermuda to Cork, if you miss the Azores and beat up and down a bit, is about 3000 nautical miles. It is one of those classic ocean passages you read about in real sailing books. A test of temperament and skill, man (and woman, of course) against the elements and all that. The city of Cork - an iconic maritime destination. We never made it.

My first transatlantic voyage was notable for several classic nautical events that seem to enshrine what everyone believes should be elements of a true fun-packed sea-going adventure (as long as one is not personally involved in the events themselves of course). Amongst other things, we even actually managed to have an infestation of weevils. They got into our rice, burrowed through our potatoes and generally ran riot through our cooks' carefully prepared inventory - since the inventory invariably involved rice and little else, we soon grew tired of picking the little blighters out of our gruel and just gave up and munched our way through some much needed protein.

As the food declined in quality, so did the weather, to such an extent that even we trainees realised that sailing was surprisingly invigorating when dangling from a yard arm suspended 80 ft up. We had rudimentary safety harnesses, of course, a belt made of webbing with a strop and 'snap shackle' attached, so we could 'clip on', as they say, to the thin metal pole (a 'Jack Stay' apparently – some nautical names are very literal) running along the top of the yard arm but, of course, you had to get to the relative safety of the yard first which involved scaling the netting up the side of the mast with the wind howling round your ears as you struggling aloft in the 'specially designed to trip you up' sailing gear. As always Frank's advice was carefully listened to.

"Don't think the harness will save you", he told us with glee, as we struggled aloft, "if you fall – it'll break your back!"

The frequency of trainees falling to their deaths was deemed sufficient to actually give it its own euphemism: "Saying hello to the deck" was a phrase much used during my time on Astrid as was "Feeding the fishes" when the new initiates regurgitated their weevil strewn supper over the side with Frank's head bobbing happily behind, encouraging us to lean further over the sides to stop "spoiling the top-sides with refuse", whatever they were. Being sick whilst aloft also provided everyone with a new and exciting distraction, dodging the unusual downpour when below or, if above, enjoying for once the relative safety of the upper yards.

Going aloft in the Caribbean was one thing whilst dressed in shorts and T-shirts but another thing entirely whilst wearing Astrid's ancient and smelly traditional 'oil skins'.

Groping for the climbing lines was made even more exciting at night since Frank had taken it upon himself to ban the use of any headlights, or indeed any lights at all when going aloft, presumably to hide the view of dark shadows falling whilst the rest of us queued up enthusiastically to attempt to control a screaming frenzied wind driven sail with only our fingernails whilst balancing precariously on the thin, single 'foot rope' beneath the yard. When my watch (Frank had carefully chosen me as watch leader possibly to maximise casualties) managed to actually snap a yard in half Frank took great delight in dispatching us aloft to attempt to lash down the broken spar with some handy sisal. As the wind howled around us and the seas crashed over the remarkably low sides of the ship I occasionally caught Frank's excited, animated gaze as he beamed up grinning madly as we manfully attempted to contain the rotten and broken pole. He was clearly enjoying the moment.

As the voyage continued the wind turned increasingly against us enabling us to discover just how effective square riggers are when sailing into the wind. They can't. Don't even think about it. You just tend to beat up and down the line hoping that something, someday will eventually change to allow you to actually make some progress. Indeed Frank's happiest day of the voyage came mid-ocean when he declared, with beaming eyes and foaming mouth, that despite our considerable efforts in tacking the cumbersome mighty beast back and forth through the previous 24 hours we had achieved only one single solitary nautical mile in a straight line towards our final destination, Cork. Practically hugging himself with joy, Frank then announced the oven had also given up the ghost and we were on cold gruel from now on. We wondered bleakly if the weevils would survive in a cold climate.

After 23 days at sea and several more gales and one storm we conceded defeat; we'd never make sunny Cork, and limped broken and wounded into Skull harbour on the south coast of Ireland at some God-awful time in the morning. I celebrated the ceremonial dropping of the anchor in the bay in appropriate fashion by immediately dry retching over the side. Having escaped sea sickness for the entire trip thus far, I took this as a good sign and clearly some kind of 'land sickness', a badge of honour for any trainee. Taking his cue, Frank immediately confined my watch and me to Harbour Duties
"Someone needs to keep an eye on the anchor and bilge" he beamed, although he was forced, failing an excuse, to release the

other stir-crazed trainees who promptly challenged themselves to a taste test of all the Irish bars in Skull. They tell me there are a lot of little Irish bars in Skull.

Having rested up for a couple of days we managed to navigate ourselves across the Irish Sea, around the rather scary Lands' End, and pulled into the delightful but surprisingly busy maritime town of Penzance. After months in the Caribbean and Bermuda we all felt rather intimidated by the people and traffic of this summer seaside resort – we just weren't used to modern life anymore and tended to form collective huddles whenever we bumped into fellow trainees ashore. By this stage we'd all taken it upon ourselves to buy the dark blue Astrid smock and we wore it religiously as a kind of tribal uniform. These sun-faded smocks helped forge a strong sense of crew unity. They also helped us pretend we were all now transatlantic-stained salty sea dogs.

The prize for the most faded and worn smock of all belonged to our long-suffering cook who had excelled herself on arrival back in the UK by deciding to not cook at all. Instead she had declared: "Sod the lot of them" and ordered a vast batch of traditional giant Cornish pasties to be delivered to the boat. The local bakery delivered them hot and ready to go. I'd never experienced a proper Cornish pasty before. Twenty six hungry trainees were plunged into silence as we demolished the huge pile of them. Wiping our mouths contentedly we all agreed it was the finest meal the Cook had produced all trip and we thanked her whole heartedly for her efforts.

The pasty had also, in my mind at least, made up for the culinary shock of that first morning in Penzance. I had begun the day, on harbour watch as always, tucking into my usual breakfast cereal only to complain bitterly to anyone bothered to hear me that there was something very wrong with the milk that morning, something very wrong indeed, it tasted funny and was less translucent than usual. I concluded that it had clearly gone off and someone's head should roll. The Cook's assistants, the 'galley rats' as they were affectionately called, informed me in no uncertain terms that that morning's milk tasted 'weird and funny' because it was something called 'fresh milk'.

"Then you should have warned me first that you were actually going to serve something 'fresh' for a change! I'm not sure my digestive systems can cope with the shock after 3 months eating round here", I shouted defiantly, attempting to save face and failing miserably. Our lugubrious Cook looked on impassively.

As we made our way slowly along the south coast the mood on board became more sombre. Despite Frank's best efforts and our many travails, we had all somehow immensely enjoyed the voyage and we knew we were now approaching journey's end, Astrid's home port, Weymouth. There, after 3 months in our company and having safely secured 3 months much needed income, Frank could finally relax and give free rein to his vitriolic hatred. Giving the traditional farewell speech to all trainees on their final day on board, Frank showed that he, too, had read the enthusiastic promises given out so long ago in the Sunday Times:

"The majority of you have underperformed on this voyage, the others" he paused dramatically, "haven't performed at all".

He then warmed to his theme, pointing out individuals that had excelled in failure, even more than the norm, whilst we looked around at each other glumly, forlornly hoping someone might offer some form of humorous defiance. I thought up several devastating ripostes, hours later, of course. So, we sat in silence. It was, after all, Frank's last kick at the cat, the moment he had been longing for, for months. Summing up, our captain concluded with characteristic flourish:

"And if you think this was an adventure of a lifetime then all I can say is", his beady eyes roamed the room, "you're going to have fuckin' miserable lives!".

MUTINY AND DEATH

The Caribbean. Antigua. A small yacht sits in the quiet confines of English Harbour. It is night.

We're lying on a hard cockpit deck and looking up at the stars as they are intermittently obscured by passing clouds. We, my new friend Jimmy and I, had decided that down below was far too hot to sleep so we have taken a side each of the partially covered cockpit outside. The teak decks are hard under elbow, but the pillows grabbed from below help. The boat is swaying ever so lightly on its mooring. As we attempt to sleep we are surrounded by the gentle sounds of the Caribbean night: a distant steel band still knocking out some tunes even though it's very late; the occasional howl of laughter or just howls emitting from a group of drunken sailors staggering away home trying to remember where the hell they left the boat; the tree frogs beep, beep, beeping away from the mango trees surrounding our sheltered little bay. We have recently returned from exploring the bars of Falmouth Bay and English Harbour itself and now, away from the relative madness of the bars, lie contentedly outside in the cooling light breeze. So, a perfect end to a tropical evening in many ways.

Jimmy lies the other side of the cockpit. I'd just met him for the first time this morning at the airport. He is older than me and, at that stage at least, far more experienced in nautical matters. So far, I hadn't learnt much about my relaxed companion other than he was employed for many years by British Telecom who'd given him a small hammer and sent him out across the country testing the telegraph poles for rot. Apparently, Jimmy would turn up in his little van, put his ear to the wooden pole, tap it, and making use no doubt of his sensitive and highly trained ears, would establish whether it needed replacing or not. He did this, he told me, for 30 years.

I assume my pole tapping friend is asleep until he suddenly stirs:

"We'll have to murder him I'm afraid" Jimmy declared.

I ponder this for a moment.

"Yes, I'm afraid that is the only reasonable course of action...it would be a blessing all round really. A mercy killing."

"Yes – put him out of his misery. An end to his suffering. He'll probably thank us after..."

"mmm, well, yes probably...if he wasn't dead and all that", I agree.

Jimmy sighs contentedly, turns over and falls asleep. Looking back that was possibly my longest continuous conversation with him. I just didn't know it then.

Of course, most crew are fine. In fact, 99% of them are. You just don't tend to remember them much though, because they're reasonable, and nice, and get on with the job in hand and don't get too drunk ashore. They're called Paul or Peter or James and come with RYA qualifications coming out of their ears. They listen, exercise sound judgement and never get angry or afraid. Those are the ones you struggle to recall when you bump into them on a pontoon years later:

"Alright mate how's it going? Oh yeh, yes, of course now what was that boat called? Yes, yes good trip. Nice one. Sorry it's....

Peter? Paul? Ah of course Dan how are you mate? Alright?" and so on. But, as I said, not all are like that.

David Brown was much older than us. Into his fifties he came with 30,000 miles of ocean experience and had been designated official boat 1st Mate. We had all gathered rather nervously at the check in desk at the allotted time in Gatwick airport earlier that morning: Alastair the highly experienced and calm skipper, Jimmy a large, quiet man who seemed affable enough although difficult to read and myself, the whipper snapper, the least experienced of all. We were one man short though and waited rather impatiently for our 1st Mate. When he did, wandering into view with his open bag slung casually over his left shoulder 40 mins late, he confidently told us he'd been in the airport for hours but had decided to find a free shower somewhere and got so carried away with scrubbing himself down that we were now rushing to check in. Not the best of first impressions I thought but Dave's second action was to decide to have a joke with security at check in who, I find, are always open to a sarcastic joke or two first thing in the morning. When asked the traditional question whether we had 'packed our bags ourselves' Dave took it upon himself to answer for us all:

"No some bloke I've never seen before packed mine for me", he declared for all to hear. The lady behind the check in desk gave him a fixed emotionless stare, sighed, and signalled security. We were all marched off 'round the back' to open and go through the contents of all our bags one by one. Once this was completed, we were routed through security and into the duty-free area.

Alistair was a non-smoker (which suited me just fine) and he had made it abundantly clear the boat would be smoke free for the duration of the voyage. Dave, undeterred by this, duly begged us all to use up our allocated duty free ration of fags for his benefit and, when reminded it was meant to be a non-smoking boat, assured us he intended to give up on the way. How buying up hundreds, perhaps thousands, of fags assisted him giving up wasn't clear at that time. And we were going a long way. Across the North Atlantic from Antigua in the Caribbean to Ardfern in Western Scotland. The English side of me found myself reluctantly agreeing so as to avoid conflict with someone I'd just met and with whom I knew I'd spend the next couple of months at sea with. My North American side would have told him to go to Hell of course. Being a fanatical non-smoker, it was the only time in my entire life that I ever bought cigarettes for anyone. If I knew what was coming, I would have volunteered to get him a couple more crates of the lethal stuff.

As we sat in the departure lounge with Dave slouched next to me chain smoking in order to give up, Jimmy seemingly engrossed in a sailing magazine and Alistair going through his carry-on bag, I felt a bit guilty for thinking poorly of our new crew mate so decided to make some idle talk to clear the smoke filled air:

"So where are you from then Dave?"

He took a long drag on his cigarette and looked at me suspiciously.

"I am a Citizen of the World" he replied. I was dimly aware of Jimmy shifting in his seat and turning a page.

"Mmm aren't we all" I grinned weakly but persisted:

"But you sound like a southerner to me, were you brought up round here?"

"You're asking this question so as to put a label on me. To put me in a box."

I staggered back a touch.

"Ehh no. Not really. Just wondering where you're from that's all."

"And once you have established THAT, you will make all sorts of incorrect and biased prejudices based upon my place of birth – as I said I am a Citizen of the World. That is all you need to know."

There was an embarrassed silence.

"Well, we've certainly established where you're from David". Opined Jimmy suddenly whilst still thumbing through his magazine. "Cuntland. That's where you're from".

Jimmy and Dave never spoke again.

Our flight was called, and we boarded. Well, all except Dave, who had decided he could squeeze one more fag in before we left. He had absorbed Jimmy's rather outspoken comment remarkably well, like water off a duck's back I thought, perhaps he was used to it? As we queued down the plane's aisle, I realised Jimmy and I had places next to each other. So, as we took our seats, I took a moment to carefully observe in a sideways fashion my intriguing, brusquely spoken companion. No emotion was apparent on his face as he casually made himself comfortable and began flipping through the onboard magazine. Alastair and Dave's seats were directly in front of us. As time went on, I noticed the plane was slowly filling up to the

gunwales and the only seat remaining empty was the one next to our increasingly flustered skipper. The minutes ticked by. The flight staff announced the plane would be leaving shortly once all passengers had boarded. There appeared to someone who had checked in but was not at the gate yet. Final calls were going out to this individual hence the 'slight' delay in our departure.
"Fingers crossed" whispered Jimmy.

Finally, just as it was clear the plane would be going and going now. Dave emerged with his bag slung casually over his shoulder strolling happily along the aisle to where Alistair was sitting. He appeared entirely unaware of the stern looks from those around him as he nestled himself into the seat directly in front of Jimmy and I. We took off. The flight attendants came round offering us drinks.

"I want tea" declared Dave as he fixed the lady with his eye. I blushed inwardly at the lack of a 'please'. My English sense of decent manners again getting the better of me. The steward fixed him with a look and silently poured him some tea. Dave took one mouthful and gave her a stern look.

"I want coffee" he said.

I fly a lot in my work and generally I find flight crew to be remarkably well trained in the arts of maintaining a calm and friendly demeanour whatever pressure is thrown at them. I have witnessed countless instances which would have any normal person foaming at the mouth and attacking customers with a full sick bag rather than smiling politely and telling them to please take their seat and the captain would be along shortly to have a 'little chat' with them. I've never seen one lose her cool quite so quickly but Dave, it appeared, had a real knack for that kind of thing.

"So, when you said 'Tea' you meant 'Coffee' then Sir?" she blurted out red faced.

"Yes, I did" smiled Dave. Another triumph.

Dave did have 30,000 sea miles under his belt though which was something I suppose. I came with next to bugger all apart from a couple of months on a square rigger. In fact, I'd never stepped aboard a yacht in my life before that day. I was really quite clueless. The skipper, Alistair Mackenzie, a remarkably pleasant man with two big shoulder bags full of experience, had accepted me on board as a third crew member because I had somehow managed to pass some Royal Yachting Association qualifications without having actually been on a yacht itself and had also survived 3 months on a square rigger with a skipper who clearly wanted me, and every other trainee on board, dead. Having landed safely in St John's airport we'd grabbed a local minibus with the obligatory deafening but fun reggae music booming out of its radio across the island to arrive down on the southern side of Antigua. The taxi drove through the walled gates of English Harbour with its remarkable, exquisite Georgian naval architecture and we went in search of our boat.

Once on board and after we'd stowed our belongings Alistair asked me to sort out a simple task:
"Could you just grab hold of the life raft down below, please Robin and stow it on the coach roof up there where we can get to it in an emergency? Me and the others are off provisioning but will be back soon".
I nodded dutifully and silently wondered what the 'life raft' looked like. I concluded it must be obvious even to a green horn like myself. I helped cast off the dingy for Alistair and the others as they pottered off in the little motorised inflatable to the local supermarket which was, then at least, admirably close to the sheltered bay we had tracked the boat down to. I briefly watched them go, armed with an impressive shopping list and Jimmy clutching an assortment of carrier bags for our precious supplies.

I went below and looked around.

'Amadea' was built in the 60's and had been maintained pretty well ever since. It hadn't been altered much though. Modernity had yet to rear its ugly head. We weren't therefore encumbered by terribly useful things like autopilots, Global Position System (GPS), fridge freezers, radar, depth or speed sounders, something called 'self-tailing' winches (which meant you actually had your hands free to use the winch itself instead of sprouting multiple hands for the same job) and so on. No this was a proper sailing boat with none of your tacky add-ons. This would be a back to basics sort of job. It was all new to me anyway. The skipper had informed me Amadea was a 42ft 'Yawl' which of course meant nothing to me then. And not much now frankly. Something to do with where the rudder is in conjunction with the stern mast apparently (Yawn) but I could see for myself that it had two masts and a couple of sails. The last and only other vessel I'd been on had had 16 different sails and 180 lines to control them. All the same colour too – this thing had multicoloured lines and everything.

Anyway I descended into the relative coolness of the saloon and looked around. The boat was in a bit of a mess but it was pretty obvious even to me that the 'life raft' was the large solid white canister sitting incongruously in the centre of the floor of the forward cabin. I had a quick look at it – it seemed to be made of two firm white shells, perhaps thick plastic or Glass Reinforced Plastic (GRP), sealed together in the middle by some sort of rubberised compound. The surfaces were smooth shiny white and the entire thing reminded me of a giant white pill. I went to lift it. The damn thing weighed a ton and had slippery solid sides with nothing to grab hold of to assist me. I decided to straddle over it, one leg on either side and haul it up and forward like some kind of human crane. Now, if you ever want to experience a proper hernia then this is definitely the way to go. I started to gamely manhandle the damn thing past the various chairs, bags, ropes and table legs in the way. Anyone lounging around their cockpits on other boats in our quiet sheltered bay would have begun to wonder what the hell was happening inside that little yawl across the way as I banged and scrapped the huge ungainly beast out of the forward cabin. It soon became apparent that the main problem, apart from its dead weight that is, was the lack of grip or any obvious purchase to be had on it. I kept finding my hands slipping away on either side of the smooth white finish, so I had another idea.

I decided to lie down and use my legs to push it physically across the floor. Lying on my back with my hands gripping the sides of the cabin doors shoving the thing with my legs worked for a bit until I noticed, between repositioning myself, a handy white line which disappeared through a little red hole in the middle seal that ran around the centre of the two joined sides. I concluded this handy line was attached no doubt to assist in carrying it. Further backing up this theory was the fact it even had a little loop tied in the end.

Getting back on my feet I slid this round my wrist and found, if I dragged the raft along the floor using the line, I could start to make really decent progress. Further-more twisting the line over my shoulder and turning my back on the thing I found it easier still, that is, until it got itself jammed between the table leg and a post. It was now late afternoon and it was hot, damn hot. Sweating profusely with the effort in the tropical heat and shouting entirely unnecessary abuse at the remarkably inanimate object I gave the line a hefty pull.

Now at this stage, with me and the life raft locked in mortal combat still within the confines of the boat's saloon, any wise and learned nautical coves reading this will expect something rather dramatic to happen. The handy little line I had discovered and had made use of to drag the raft across the floor was not installed to assist in carrying it but in setting the bloody thing off. It was the equivalent of the rip cord on a parachute, the fuse on the bomb, the line of powder to the keg of dynamite which in this case was directly connected to a ruddy great cylinder of gas primed to inflate the huge life raft in seconds. As I heroically gave the line one last almighty heave I, and everyone else floating in that tranquil bay, was blissfully unaware of what was about to happen next.

The line parted. I fell backwards and crashed into the companion way stairs with the end of the painter still clutched in my sweaty palms. The white beast just sat there, still jammed behind the table leg, mocking my feeble efforts. As I lay there I inspected with disgust the parted end and discarded it in frustration and went back to carrying along as best I could, dragging it up the companion way stairs and then installing it as instructed on the coach roof cradle. Grabbing some spare webbing I secured it down and sat back rather pleased with my efforts whilst ruminating on the thought these things should really come with some kind of transport strops. That little handling line was just rubbish.

Soon after Alistair and company returned with a boat load full of grub and the rest of the afternoon was taken up finding space below for sacks of onions, peppers, fruit, rice, potatoes, covering eggs in Vaseline (apparently it helped keep them fresh) and finding somewhere to stow a small mountain of cans. The broken and entirely useless little raft 'carry line' went right out of my head. It was only the next morning, before we set sail on the first little leg of 2000 miles or so to the Azores that it came back to me.

"Mmm Al? I forgot to mention that little line on the life raft. It parted yesterday and now there's only this little stub left." I pointed to the tiny bit of line still sticking out of the raft.

I noticed Alastair's eyes bulged a bit but he kept admirably calm. Giving me a little sideways re-assessing kind of look, Al made it clear we'd have to take the thing back to the local chandlery – apparently it had just been 'serviced' and they clearly hadn't done a very good job. I whole heartedly agreed though I had no idea what he was talking about and volunteered to help him manhandle the treacherous thing into our little dinghy and we motored over to the local store that had organised the service.

It was only when Al slammed the thing down on the desk there and declared that the guy that had serviced this 'should be shot' that the penny finally began to drop. Al went on:
"It was only when my crew here gave the inflation painter a little test pull" the man behind the counter raised one eyebrow "that this happened!" and he showed him the snub of painter left sticking out. We all agreed it was shocking and someone's head should roll whilst I privately tried to imagine what would have happened if I'd actually managed to set off a six man life raft within the confines of the tiny saloon within a 42ft yawl. Of course, it then slowly dawned on me that I had, in fact, actually saved the day. I mean, what would have happened if we were sinking and we lashed this 'painter line' down, gave it a pull to inflate only to the see the end part and watch our life raft happily drift away as our boat sank beneath us? Upon reflection I took no small amount of pride in the fact that luckily we had on board a member of crew so cluelessly imbecilic that he was mad enough to test whether the life raft would actually inflate or not under duress whilst still indoors.

Returning to the vessel we now had a bit more time free to see a little bit of English Harbour and its environs whilst our life raft was re-serviced. With the lull in our activity, David took the opportunity to request a favour of me. Having bought several postcards, he now asked me to fill them out and send them for him. He instructed me to send one to his parents and another to some sister or other back in Ireland. He told me I was to write something about how we had formed into a brave band of brothers already and how beautiful Antigua was. Puzzled by this request I tentatively suggested that his parents and family would be more receptive to a postcard from him, their son and brother, rather than a complete stranger. He dismissed this observation with a wave of his hand. I persisted:

"But why don't you write to them Dave? They're you're parents not mine!"

"Me?" he responded, "oh I can't be bothered with all that crap".

At least he was honest I suppose.

That evening we ate on board and afterwards Jimmy and I jumped into the dinghy hoping to get away before Dave noticed we were going for a drink ashore. Al had already elected to stay on board. As we crept down into the little inflatable as quietly as we could 'sshing' each other Dave emerged out of nowhere.

"You going ashore?"

"Huh, yes just for a couple of drinks we'll catch you later."

"I'm coming too." he declared and jumped in.

"Eh, of course" I mumbled. Jimmy gave me a reproachful look.

The rest of the evening we toured the handful of bars dotted around the marina before venturing across the thin peninsula separating English Harbour to Falmouth Bay. At each one, and as the local rum punches took hold, David became more and more outspoken in his criticism of our skipper, his doubts about the boat, route, provisioning, weather and our obvious lack of abilities as fellow sailors. Luckily, he declared, he was on board to save our worthless skins. For his part Jimmy took all this remarkably equably, silently sipping his rum punch and looking round contentedly, clearly just enjoying being in the relative cool of the Caribbean night. Coming from the cold and damp UK in early Spring there was something wonderful about just being able to sit outside in shorts and T shirt in the evening sipping a cool drink. The heat of the day was over. Now the intense tropical sun was down the temperature ashore was pretty much perfect. Falmouth Harbour stretched out before us, people on holiday passing to and fro, yachties, locals all mixing in together with the twinkling lights of hundreds of little boats at anchor in the large bay before us. Heaven on Earth I thought.

"God, I hate this tacky place" announced Dave so we went home.

The next morning, having retrieved our re-serviced life raft with shiny new painter attached which this time I decided not to test, we pottered the boat over to the fuel dock straight across the other side of our little bay. Half-way there I looked astern and noticed our dinghy happily floating away. Dave had tied it on so badly that it had immediately taken the opportunity to make a break for freedom. Alistair was not impressed as we did an about face and picked it up. It occurred to me, David and I were locked into some form of death struggle over who on board could be the most incompetent. I had started well but Dave was quickly catching up.

As we motored out to sea David took it upon himself to take me under his wing and show me 'the ropes'. Being entirely clueless, I was more than happy to take instruction from anyone. The first lesson was a surprise though since it appeared to involve taking all your clothes off. We were barely out of sight of the bars ashore before David stripped off and showed us all how to urinate into the sea without leaving the cockpit – all you needed to do, he demonstrated, was to kneel on the edge of the coaming and piss directly into the wind. As your bodily fluid happily splatters the teak decks and blows back into your face, you'll get a good, indeed graphic idea, of both wind strength and direction. I digested this lesson without comment and decided to keep my clothes on for the present.

Next, and still in his 'birthday suit', Dave took me forward to where the mainsail halyard lived and gave me a lesson in the perils of using a winch. Having only sailed on square riggers I had never used a 'winch' before and was keen to see how a pro used these powerful devices. Dave wrapped the mainsail halyard several times round the winch on the mast and begun heaving on the line that in turn pulled the mainsail up the track on the mast. As the sail slid up and began flapping in the breeze, it was clear more power was needed. He then showed me how to take several more turns around the winch, insert the winch handle and begin grinding the rest of the big sail up. Straddling the winch, his legs on either side with his testicles dangling within inches of the heavily powered up steel halyard, I found my eyes inexplicably began to water. Although I had no desire to observe Dave's most precious parts up close or indeed at all, I found it impossible to divert my eyes from the slow moving but hideous catastrophe that was playing itself out remorselessly before me. With Dave, naked as the day he was born, grunting and sweating away with the effort of it all, the steel halyard itself began to squeal under the considerable load as his scrotum sack rocked gently back and forth, occasionally just touching, toying, with the top of the rotating squealing winch. As the load increased Dave began to sweat profusely and moved his position ever closer to the powered up rotating drum leaving his fearless gonads dangling inches from the screaming furious beast, I found I just couldn't take it anymore and had to look away to the distant horizon.

The scream echoed around Freeman's Bay. I turned in horror to find our heroic 1st Mate rolling in naked agony beneath the winch clutching his nether regions with both hands. As he rocked gently back and forth moaning, Alastair bravely established Dave had only lost a couple of pubes to the winch and all other 'equipment' was, in fact, still happily intact. By which I assumed he meant the 'winch' was just fine. Upon reflection it was an unusual way of starting a long ocean voyage but we all agreed the incident had clearly had an impact upon the general morale on board. I can still see Jimmy's beaming happy face even today. Mind you, it was the best safety lesson I ever got.

We had largely light winds and calm seas for much of the long slow leg to Horta in the Azores. At first, we sailed towards the North to pick up, in theory at least, the traditionally prevailing Westerlies that would blow us to Europe but this year they never really showed up. Instead we took what breeze we could when we could. Hand steering the entire way Al set up a watch system that kept us organised and allowed plenty of down time between taking our 'trick' at the helm. From early on, Dave used his time off to 'carry out improvements to the boat' as he declared. Observing his efforts from a safe distance most of his improvements seem to revolve around attaching numerous bungee cords to pretty much everything he could get his hands on. Soon these little trip wires were everywhere and their main aim, it seemed to me at least, was to irritate and annoy our long-suffering skipper. Having transformed the cockpit and saloon into some form of bizarre nautical cobweb with Dave, presumably, sitting spider-like in the middle he turned his attention to the galley. The oven had been working just fine heating up food and staying hot as required, doing what ovens do in other words, but Dave 'improved' it to such an extent that after he had finished the poor thing was only any use as a reserve cupboard, its happy days of actually working long forgotten. He moved on to navigation and was soon declaring we were clearly going the wrong way and issuing orders countermanding those of our remarkably composed skipper. On deck he got the sails set up so wrong that he cut a sizeable tear in the main which we then had to drop to stitch back together. Alistair, perhaps run down by Dave's constant complaining, took to his cabin with a migraine.

As we drifted around repairing the sail David took Jimmy and I aside to explain his plan. In a conspiratorial whisper he advised us that, with Alistair lying motionless and in obvious distress in his bunk, he was clearly incapable of skippering the boat and we needed to take action. In short this was our chance to mutiny. We (by which he meant him, of course) needed to take the ship over so as to avoid 'inevitable disaster'. Jimmy and I had no idea what 'disaster' Dave had in mind other than the obvious one of having him take charge. One of many reasons for our doubts surrounding Dave's plan was that he had clearly picked up far too fond a love of the owner's whisky. Although the skipper had made it abundantly clear this was a dry boat and no one was to touch the owners spirits, each night I woke to hear the tell-tale tingling of glass on glass and the sipping of contraband in the wee hours. Perhaps this was all part of Dave's plan to give up booze along with the smoking?

Another evening, perhaps inspired by his love of strong spirits, I awoke to hearing Dave calling up a passing cargo vessel requesting the clearly puzzled 2nd Officer onboard to 'throw a crate of bananas' over for us since we were short of fruit. The non-plussed officer responded that since it was night, it may prove difficult to find, whereupon Dave suggested attaching a light of some form to help isolate said crate of bananas. Why Dave thought the cargo boat had such a huge and easily convenient crate of bananas to hand is still a mystery to me. The officer politely demurred that he had no banana-tossing assistants at hand that evening and must now, sadly, return to his duties (to escape this crazy Englishman, I assume). Either way we were not about to hand control of the boat over to a banana-crazed, whisky-swilling loon who possessed all the personality traits capable of starting a fight in an empty room.

In less than 24 hours Dave's mutiny was a thing of the past; Alastair had fully recovered, Jimmy had done a grand job repairing the main and even the wind began to play along, allowing our little boat to start making good speed for once towards its destination. Unfortunately, as is so often the case in sailing, we went from too little wind to too much. And then, far too much. With the increasing wind came the rain, small little slurries at first, then more consistent as the front approached. This prompted us to reach for our newly acquired 'wet weather gear' and, as we struggled into our proud new costumes, Jimmy and I eyed each other's new apparel with interest. It was immediately apparent we had both gone for major leading brands with their whizz bang all breathable, super durable Gortex wonder of modern science approach to keeping us dry. These garments shared several outstanding characteristics. Both manufacturers had come up with the sort of techno jargon that takes your breath away and dulls the mind – it was all ultra-wicking semi-permeable membranes of magic fairy dust with T5YXE coating providing a resistance level up to super hurricane conditions and so on and so forth which, of course, meant nothing to either of us. Another shared characteristic, we soon established, was that we had both parted with a small fortune for these sea defying wonders of modern science plus we were soon to discover one more common trait. Neither actually kept you dry.

As the wind and rain started to really hammer down, it was all good at first and we enjoyed watching the small little droplets run like crazy down the super aqua-phobic material but then, as we sat in a happy puddle of rainwater mixed with salt water, it eventually became apparent that slowly getting a wet arse was also a feature of our ultra-modern breathable kit. Then Alastair came up to help. He was dressed in what appeared to be oilskins he'd discovered in a Christmas cracker. They were made of shiny plastic, bright sky blue, thin as you like and were 100% waterproof. He finished off the look with a pair of yellow 'marigold' dishwashing gloves that provided not only complete aridity of hands but also truly excellent grip on the helm too. I think he picked them up at Tesco's for a quid.

As we sat in our respective puddles, slowly becoming aware of the seeping ingress into our state-of-the-art salopettes, Alastair launched into one of his quite remarkable sea-faring tales. For once though I wasn't listening attentively since my mind had wandered back to the conversation I'd had with the salesperson a month or so previously in the chandlery I had purchased my super expensive sailing gear. Being a novice in these matters I'd ask her to explain the various coding they'd put on their products to help me understand the enormous rising costs of each jacket on a single long rack. The salesperson had happily taken the opportunity to practise what they'd no doubt just learnt at a recent product sales course:

"Well I'm glad you asked." She cried whilst grabbing the first jacket on the rack, clearly a light weight one but boasting a seriously heavyweight price tag. "The TA1 is our lightest breathable sailing jacket for short coastal hops with resistance levels of up to 2 hours in moderate inclement weather."

I looked at her blankly but managed to nod wisely whilst moving down the rack.

"And the TA2?" I queried.

"The TA2 is for more ambitious offshore sailing and is guaranteed to keep you dry for up to 4 hours". She gave me a quick appraising look.

"It's for serious sailors" she added apologetically. Moving down the line of jackets I silently digested this information whilst trying to hide the fact that my mind was racing in confusion. Approaching the end of the rack I picked out a more expensive garment still. I would need a mortgage for this one, but it did look really cool with lots of cuffs and high collars and Velcro everywhere.

"Ah, the TA3 is our ocean-going jacket, top of the range using our toughest fabric yet it'll keep you dry, warm and cosy for up to an unbelievable 6 hours!". I looked at her in confusion and, being pretty new to this game, asked a really daft question:
"Mmm that sounds great, but do you have anything that is...well...waterproof?"

As the sea and breeze picked up with dark clouds flying overhead, we soon found ourselves staggering dangerously around the coach roof putting in the 1st Reef, then 2nd then our 3rd and final Reef. As mentioned Amadea was a proper old-fashioned sailing vessel which meant when you had to reduce sail it meant putting yourself at maximum risk rather than the other way round. As the waves grew in size and stature Dave's resolve and determination seemed to reduce accordingly. By the time we found ourselves in our first proper gale our 1st Mate was reduced to a simpering wreck staggering around quietly praying to himself, apologising to all for everything and nothing, shaking uncontrollably and eventually taking to his bunk in sheer terror. Well, I should say, 'taken' to his bunk would be more accurate, by Jimmy in fact, who had found him that night, in a panic, desperately climbing the mast in just his pants without lifejacket or harness. Jimmy has stridden forward, pulled him down, gave him 'a little friendly tap' and manhandled him safely below. Upon reflection none of us were quite sure what he was looking for up there…perhaps a hidden cache of cigarettes? The last bottle of the owners whisky? Or even his last banana perhaps?

I must confess, being pretty new to this game myself, I didn't find this behaviour too reassuring though I noticed that both the skipper and my newfound buddy Jimmy appeared totally unfazed by the roaring and screaming outside. So, having spent many hours fighting the helm myself, I took the opportunity to get my head down whilst I could. Even Dave's whimpering and rocking back and forth in the bunk next to mine didn't keep me awake – I guess I should have been more sympathetic but, to be honest, I was just too knackered to care.

When I awoke early the next morning it was to a boat now eerily quiet. At first I put this down to the fact Dave's sobbing had evidently ceased but then, as I looked beyond the covers of my sleeping bag it was clear we still had big seas outside and the wind was still blowing hard but our little boat just seemed to be bobbing happily up and down with the sea, not fighting it anymore, just going with it. Looking up I noticed the

helm had been lashed securely down and looking outside all the sails were down and stowed securely on deck. Seeing me awake Alastair, dressed is his cheap as you like and therefore actually waterproof 'oilskins' gave me a big grin and said:
"We're hove to Robin."
I frowned.
"Drop the sails, lash the helm to windward and the boat can look after itself, doesn't need our help other than keeping a lookout and it lets you lot get some sleep".
I looked across at Dave. Being 'hove to' certainly seemed to work for him. Even our heroic 1st Mate had given up the fight and was now snoring contentedly.

It took us 21 days at sea to get to the Azores from Antigua. This is not fast going although I've no doubt plenty of boats have done it slower. A lot more have done it quicker though. By the time we pulled up alongside the cheerfully multicoloured painted walls of Horta Jimmy and I were fairly gagging to escape the confines of Amadea (and its 1st Mate). It was late afternoon. As we secured the vessel, Alastair gave us one look and a knowing nod, and we literally ran down the dock to the nearest bar. We ordered a couple of beers and took a seat beside a window overlooking the marina. Being a Portuguese island two Superbok beers soon emerged. We toasted our good fortune for having survived so far and took a comforting swig. Then we saw Dave wandering down the road clearly looking for us. Now I know this is immature and I can't say it fills me with pride to confess this many years later but we did actually hide under the table as he approached our window and went past only emerging when the coast was clear. The barman gave us a queer look and shrugged.

'Bloody yachties. All the same.' he seemed to say.

Jimmy and I were expecting Alistair to basically throw Dave off the boat in Horta. Equally likely, or so we hoped, would be that Dave would throw himself off. When neither occurred, Jimmy and I contemplated throwing Dave off the boat ourselves or at least off the pier but that didn't happen either, so only two days later we found ourselves casting off our lines, taking one last look at our painting on the floor on the marina and pointed our bows towards southern Ireland. Dave had announced that, with regret, he would leave us in Ireland and go 'visit his sister if she still lived there'. Hearing these inspiring words, we set every scrap of sail we had and cracked on as fast as we could and, for once, we made good progress.

A week later we found ourselves approaching Wicklow in the early evening with Jimmy steering and me checking our position and simply enjoying looking at the Irish coast from our little cockpit. We had full sails out, that's both of them, and several hours of daylight left to get in and say farewell to our 1st Mate. Alastair was catnapping below while he had the chance before taking charge of our approach. Dave came up the companionway steps, sat down and suddenly launched into a story:

"When we were in that storm, I know I behaved..." a pause "...not particularly well".

Jimmy's eyes bulged slightly but we both stayed quiet expecting there was more to come. There was.

"Many years ago, I became a delivery skipper too, just like Alastair. I was living down in Australia and I was given a job delivering a boat to Tasmania. I had two crew, both pretty inexperienced, one a complete novice."

I shuffled in my seat uncomfortably. I had a premonition I knew what was coming.

"It's not a particularly long run but I forgot to check the weather before we left. I should have done but I'd been busy sorting things out on the engine before we left, I can't help wondering now if I left something turned off. Either way it was fine before I started but wasn't when we needed it most. We got going and of course the weather turned bad."

He looked at us uncomfortably.

"Then it got very bad. Soon we were in real trouble and, when I checked our position, I realised we were being swept down on to some reefs. There's plenty around there you know. When we saw the breakers one crew, the novice, went below to hide. I tried to start the engine but got nothing. Can't help thinking it must have been something I'd done. Anyway, the engine wouldn't start, and we tried but couldn't sail out of it. We hit the reef."

We both stared at Dave. He went quiet for a bit. Amadea was sailing along nicely now with the evening sun turning her sails a slight glowing red. The green fertile coast of Ireland looked even more alluring in this half-light.

"When we hit the reef, we began to sink. One of the crew was still on deck with me. I shouted to him that we needed to get the life raft off the coach roof, and I called down to the guy down below to come up and help but he refused. He was too terrified, you see." Dave looked up at us pathetically.

"The boat began to break up and was swaying around on the rocks. I climbed up on the coach roof. With the sail down the boom was swinging around like crazy. As I started to untie the life raft the boom swung over and knocked me into the water."

Amadea heeled over a touch and Jimmy turned slightly downwind to ease the pressure on the sails. The coast of Ireland was clear on our port beam. I looked at the rocks on the coast. Dave continued:

"The water's pretty warm around there in summer you know. An hour or so later, I don't know, difficult to keep track of time, I washed up on the beach. The boat went down. As it sank the raft somehow managed to break free and miraculously inflated. Guess the painter was attached and as the boat sank dragging the life raft with it, it was pulled tight, inflated the raft and then parted under the load. The one lad... the one with me outside, managed to swim over and get into it alright. He was picked up several hours later. Guess someone spotted it floating around."

Dave went silent. Jimmy sat emotionless, apparently concentrating on his helming. The wind whistled gently in the rigging.

"And the other crew. The novice. What happened to him?" I asked.

"Oh, him?" replied Dave looking morosely at his feet "He went down with the ship".

In Wicklow we said farewell and went for a beer. We found the nearest watering hole and Al ordered three Guinness's. No one spoke. The drinks turned up and Al made a little toast gesture, raising his glass slightly to the sky, which we copied. We sat together in companionable silence at the bar. Drinks finished we left and crossed the street. As we strolled back towards the marina, I noticed a minor disturbance at the bus stop where we'd left Dave. His plan was to turn up unannounced at his sister's place but was unsure of the reception he'd receive so thought he'd just turn up out of the blue and see how it went. He planned to get the local bus to her village. We spotted him on the bus. There was a small crowd of people queuing up behind Dave who appeared to be in the middle of some heated argument with the bus driver. The people behind him looked rather put out. We all subconsciously hastened our pace a touch and scurried past.

Safely round the corner and on our way back to the boat Jimmy leaned over conspiratorially:

"Told you we should have murdered him" he said evenly.

HURRICANES AND OTHER INCONVENIENT THINGS

It is high summer in the stunningly beautiful French Riviera.

I had been kicking my heels in the coolly chic and therefore massively expensive town of Beaulieu sur Mer, whilst attempting to break into the highly paid and therefore highly desirable super yacht industry. I hadn't broken in very far. Infact not at all. Earlier in the year a well-respected and worldly wise instructor at the illustrious United Kingdom Sailing Academy had packed me and a Scottish colleague off to France reassuring me that the sailing industry was crying out for heavily qualified (on paper at least) crew like myself.

"They'll be falling over each other in the scrum to sign you up on lucrative contracts for multi-billion-pound yachts. Mark my words" he said "with qualifications like yours all you'll need to do" he leaned closer, dropping his voice conspiratorially "is rock up at the Blue Lady Pub in Antibes, that's where they all go, wave your Long Range Radio Certificate in the air and they'll be scrambling across the bar to buy you a beer, cosy up to you, get you drunk and you'll be signed up and living the life of Riley before you even sober up" he finished with a wink.

It hadn't quite worked out like that. A couple of weeks later, sitting feeling rather foolish in the Blue Lady Pub in Antibes we had sipped a couple of beers counting the last of our shekels, been ignored by all and sundry apart from a local yacht agent who had spent many hours extolling the difficulties and impossibilities of gaining employment in 'the Industry' as she called it. Apparently unless you were under 25, stunningly gorgeous and preferably female you had no chance. Since I was none of these things, we had finished our beers and promptly resolve to take the bull by the horns and give up. My Scottish companion had caught the next flight back to Edinburgh leaving me ruing the day I ever thought about sailing the high seas for a living. Apparently, I was too old, too ugly and too male.

A couple of days later, as I was dolefully packing my bags, a friend of mine came to the rescue however with the offer of an unpaid but at least free trip home on a yacht delivery.

"You get on the boat, check everything over, sail it from Antibes to Southampton with food thrown in and voila you get home for free!" he said. I jumped onboard and several weeks later found myself kicking my heels back in the UK for a change. With few other avenues open to me, and now contemplating this new and exciting world of 'yacht delivery', I contacted a large well-known firm and offered my services.

My experiences thus far had caused a realignment with reality so I wasn't surprised to hear no skipper jobs of course, or even 1st Mate positions (far too inexperienced apparently) but there WAS a brand new catamaran sitting in La Coruna in NW Spain that was looking for a couple of crew to assist in taking it to a place called 'Deltaville'. I was told the new boat had had an 'interesting' trip from the Sables D'Olonne only 250 miles away on the other side of Biscay and was now lying in the marina there patiently awaiting the arrival of replacement skipper and crew. Since I had nothing else to do, I signed up. It was August and I had no idea where 'Deltaville' was, but I didn't like to look ignorant in front of the office so hadn't asked. I mean, surely everyone in sailing knows where 'Deltaville' is? A month later, as I quietly contemplated my own mortality or loss thereof, it occurred to me I really should have asked.

La Coruna is one of those magnificent Spanish cities that no one ever really goes to. You may have heard of it of course, in passing, or at least pretend to have heard of it whilst looking sagely out the window sipping your Spanish brandy sighing dramatically "Ah yes, bonita La Coruna" and then smile secretly. But no one actually goes there. You should though. Especially in June when the whole ancient quarter of the city turns itself into a Medieval Fair with fire breathing jugglers, huge vats of sizzling meats, jesters, locals dressed up in elaborate costumes, dragons, tumblers, acrobats and bemused drunken yacht crew staggering around in the middle of it all wondering what the hell is going on.

When we arrived there, however, the festival was just a distant memory, it was August remember, and we headed straight for the marina in the centre of town. After boarding the brand new 44ft catamaran several things were immediately apparent. It was fair to say the initial leg from the Sables D'Olonne had obviously not been incident free. The mainsail cover, a thick bag that the sail drops into, was in tatters, the reefing lines used to shorten the main had parted in various places, the other sail at the front, the jib, had a hole punched through it, the boat batteries appeared drained beyond redemption, and the safety guardrails that run around deck of the 2 hulls, to help trip you up and over the edge, had been ripped clean away. Inside we discovered a half empty and remarkably large carafe of super cheap wine and a note from the previous skipper wishing us 'bon voyage' for the 'next little leg' to Deltaville. Since the vessel had only logged 250 miles and was barely weeks old we were all quietly impressed by the amount of carnage achieved in such a short space of time and distance; this skipper must have been a real salty sea dog from the good old days of sailing. The days before GPS for instance, weather forecasts, insurance, sailing qualifications and any form of prudence or self-restraint whatsoever.

Our skipper, a highly experienced salty old sea dog himself, soon had us sorting out all these problems and getting the boat ready for the next leg. We were joined by his mate and officially our '1st Mate' John, a recently retired senior police officer from the Isle of Wight and Barbarella, a tall leggy Dutch girl with enormous blue eyes and crazy frizzled blond hair.

"We need to get this mess sorted out before we leave for Sao Miguel. I want to get going tomorrow and we've a long way to go, it's a good 850 miles away" the skipper declared. Everyone else nodded sagely.

I frowned "Sao Miguel?"

The Skipper and 1st Mate, perhaps noticing me for the first time, now scrutinised me with renewed interest. We'd only just met on the plane and, once it had been established that I'd recently 'qualified' from the United Kingdom Sailing Academy, they had looked at me with something bordering on contempt. Which I thought was fair enough.

"Fast track, eh?" John had said looking at me pityingly and they had continued their discussions on baggy wrinkling and handy billies ignoring me for the rest of the journey.

"Sao Miguel in the Azores of course, from there it's a couple of thousand miles to the harbour at St George's" the Skipper confirmed.

I looked blank.

"That's Bermuda to you, before the final leg, 700 miles or so to Chesapeake Bay…that's if we get across 'the Wall' OK…." he trailed off into silent introspection.

Barbarella and I looked at each other.

"So, Deltaville is in... the United States then?".

The Skipper nodded, too overcome by our ignorance, to summon up the energy to elucidate further.

"Little place in Virginia up the Chesapeake Bay" added John with a reassuringly smile.

That evening, after dinner ashore and much fine Spanish vino I stood on the bow slightly woozy pondering the journey ahead. It was late August, so I calculated we'd be well into September by the time we'd get to these 'Azores' the Skipper was banging on about. A thought sparked into life. I dimly remembered an 'Introduction to Astro-Navigation' lecture I had wandered absent-mindedly into at the Sailing Academy the previous year. The purpose of the lecture was to valiantly attempt to persuade us Academy students that sextants weren't old fuddy-duddy things that went out with the Ark; they were in fact sexy and modern and that astro-navigation was definitely the next BIG THING in sailing, so I should splash out 500 precious quid for my 'Ocean Ticket' as they called it.

"Forget your GPS, DECCA, Quadrants and Falstaff's" said the lecturer, desperately punting for business for his 3-week course, "It's all about declination, noon sights and Azimuths" he blathered as I found my eyes slowly glazing over. The rest of the pitch was all lost on me but now, standing on the gently shifting bow of the boat overlooking the inner harbour of La Coruna, I did vaguely recall an interesting bar graph slide showing monthly Atlantic hurricane frequency (or 'Tropical Revolving Storms', advised the cash strapped lecturer, which sounded much more scientific and therefore less scary). I dimly recollected September had the biggest bar by far on the bar graph, in fact, it was twice the size of all the others. I shrugged. No doubt the skipper knows best. Salty sea dog and all that.

It didn't take long for rough weather to find us. A couple of days out and heading southwest we soon found ourselves in high seas with a tiny scrap of jib out to keep us moving forward. The waves were particularly impressive at night, thundering down on us out of the darkness, the breaking white foam visible beyond the blue/black chaos of the sea. John, the 1st Mate, was soon struck down by sea sickness as we surfed our way to the target. I remained strangely well and fairly content to watch wave after wave bearing down on us in frenzied anger. I guess I kept reminding myself it wasn't personal, the sea didn't mean it, it was just, well, doing its thing, that's all.

Having successfully survived the watch trying to 'get your head down' in your bunk was another thing entirely. The noise down below was simply atrocious. On catamarans, the first hull to encounter the wave tends to rise up with it leaving the befuddled monster nowhere to go except to smash into the 2nd hull. Rather than move with the waves cats tend to resist them. This creates a problem. Each impact shakes you and the boat to its core. I could go on but sailing books are full of these tedious descriptions of mighty seas towering above the brave and fearless narrator as he or she struggles to do something incomprehensible with a shackle and a spare toothbrush.

If you are keen to experience this yourself however it's possible to simulate the general effects in the comfort of your own home so you too can feel like a proper sailor without the constant opportunity of drowning. All you need to do is move to the epicentre of an extremely active earthquake zone, acquire one of those clever nursing beds they have in hospitals with electric motors all over them and then recruit a strong and able neighbour who's handy with a sledgehammer. When you feel the first tremors coming, jump into bed, take the break off the wheels, attach electrodes to the electric motor controlling the bed sending it into uncontrollable spasms, whilst politely asking your sympathetic neighbour to repeatedly but also (and this is important) randomly bash the side of your house with his sledgehammer. As you whizz round your bedroom ricocheting off the walls whilst being deafened by the enthusiastic efforts of your friendly neighbour, you'll be able to get a small sensation of what it actually feels like trying to sleep in heavy weather on a small boat at sea. Keep this simulation going for as long as possible (you may need to give your neighbour a break and a nice cup of tea occasionally). Just bear in mind you'll have to get up for your watch again in a couple of hours.

Several days later, broken and beaten yet again (as is the Great Tradition of the Sea) we limped into Sao Miguel on the island of Ponta Delgado, the capital of the Portuguese owned islands of the Azores. The Azores are one of those great secrets of the sea. A stunningly verdant chain of volcanic islands erupting out of the centre of the northern Atlantic these islands truly are a welcome sight to all sailors who make land fall there. The people are friendly and generous, the ports and harbours organised and efficient and each island offers a new and pleasantly unique experience. On top of this you can sail from one to another just by pointing your bow at it and still get in by beer o'clock. A sailors' paradise in other words and we just didn't want to leave. Well, except John, who did, after a week of chucking up and being thrown around, he'd had enough. Besides John was an experienced sailor with an 'Ocean ticket' and he'd looked at the weather, sniffed the air, turned around 3 times and didn't like what he saw.

The first hurricane came out of hiding whilst we were still in the Azores. I thought that quite polite of it since it gave us an opportunity to delay a little longer there. The Skipper, however, decided that we could at least make some progress west, so we set sail for the little island of Faial a day or so away. Faial's main town, Horta, is a true sailing Mecca since it is the home, I was told, of the most famous sailing bar in the world. You've never heard of it, of course, and neither had I, but Peter's Cafe Sport is a proper job watering hole with locals happily rubbing shoulders with nautical coves in a friendly convivial setting as no doubt the blurb goes. It's a good place to get drunk and bore everyone stupid with your sailing stories in other words. We did just that for several days as we observed the hurricane tracking across the ocean well to the south of us and beyond our route. After a couple of days, the Skipper declared it was now safe to go and also announced, now that former 1st Mate John had fled, that I had been duly promoted to the coveted position of 1st Mate. Barbarella looked worried.

We set sail and, once we had covered sufficient territory to make a return to the Azores implausible, the next hurricane duly popped up on the weather reports. This one was a real beauty too, hundreds of miles across and steadily building, it was currently rampaging its way westwards from its birthplace near the Cape Verde islands well to our southeast. We contemplated the ramifications. If it began to start shifting northwards it would probably continue to curve round, speed up and charge towards the northeast. The question was when and where would it begin this re-curvature? We decided that rather than head straight towards Bermuda, which would probably bring us face to face with the beast, we'd run north-westwards whilst monitoring the position of the hurricane, hoping that it would recurve and pass safely beneath us. Then we could make towards Bermuda. That was the plan and it was a good one too. Until the second hurricane popped up and started 'heading us off at the pass' by making its way up from the Caribbean towards Bermuda. So, as we manfully ran away north-westwards, we had one hurricane coming up behind us from the southeast and now another one heading towards us from the southwest. In layman's terms we were the jam in a hurricane sandwich. An analogy I kept to myself at the time.

Luckily, we had several big blue hardbound serious looking and therefore ball-crushingly dull Admiralty books on board about sailing the world's oceans. Up until now I had happily ignored their very existence. No longer. I frantically grabbed one from a shelf and looked up the section on 'Tropical Revolving Storms'. I learnt that even hurricanes themselves had categories (as if being a ruddy great hurricane wasn't enough someone had to go and rate them for viciousness). I discovered that there are no less than 5 different categories of boat-breakingly aggressive hurricanes. The 'least' i.e. only insanely aggressive, is Category 1, the 'worst' i.e. description defyingly unpleasant, is Category 5. I double checked the weather advisory. Both hurricanes had been listed as Category 5. We were doomed.

The next morning, as I attempted to make a stolid, lumpy little cruising cat achieve world beating speeds in what was, for the moment at least, light winds, Barbarella joined me companionably on watch. She sat quietly observing me for a while, coolly puffing away on her ubiquitous cigarettes, as I made frantic and utterly fruitless efforts to achieve another nano digit of speed.

"I'd be enjoying this trip if it wasn't for all these hurricanes", she said airily with a smile as she brushed her crazy wind tossed hair to one side. I paused from my efforts looking up at her incredulously as she continued:

"What do you think we'll do if one catches up with us?"

Her large blue eyes bulged at me. I paused frantically searching for some meaningless but reassuring words of comfort. Suddenly I remembered my days in the Cub Scout Association:

"I guess we'll just do our best" I said lamely.

I didn't continue with the rest about Duty, God, the Queen and keeping the Cub Scout law. Perhaps I should have done? Barbarella seemed satisfied anyway and bounced off leaving me pondering the same question. On this boat in a Category 5 hurricane? Fifty percent chance perhaps, maybe with a bit of luck thrown in? I wondered how my family would mourn my passing. How the great sailing community would bemoan the loss of such talent so early in so promising a career. I wondered if we'd even make the Stroud News and Journal? Small boats at sea. Out of sight and out of mind. I resolved that I had, if I survived, learnt a very important sailing lesson. Namely, don't try to sail from Europe to America via the North Atlantic in September. It is a very silly thing to do. Very silly indeed.

We survived, of course. The hurricane behind us recurved as we had hoped passing safely astern of us and charging off towards the UK. To our front the other Category 5 hurricane was one of those murderous ones described simply by meteorologists as 'erratic'. Instead of hunting us down and, most probably, wiping us out it decided to do a 270 degree turn and flew off at 20 knots to destroy the northeast coast of America instead. We had escaped.

Finally, many days later, we found ourselves pottering gently into St George's in Bermuda. Having resisted the strong temptation to throw myself on the ground kissing the dock we were soon approached by a gregarious local:
"So, who are these crazy guys crossing the Atlantic this time of year?! Man, you must be mad for sure!", he said with a big welcoming grin. Our salty sea dog of a Skipper found himself agreeing with him and promptly booked the first flight home to England. The plane left the next morning. Before leaving however he announced that I had been promoted again, this time

to 'skipper' with Barbarella now elevated to the lofty heights of 1st Mate.

"Don't let me down" he said.

We were still 800 miles from Deltaville. And now there were just two of us.

Barbarella and I sat in St George's for a while watching yet another hurricane track its way across the Atlantic beneath us. It was a particularly busy month for hurricanes even by September's busy standards. Once it was finally safe to leave, we got going again and, after carefully navigating our little cat round the enormous reefs surrounding Bermuda's northern shores, shaped course for the entrance to Chesapeake Bay 700 miles away. The rotational watch system was now 4 hours on and 4 hours off. Before fleeing, our erstwhile skipper had handed over his chart pack for the rest of the voyage assuring me that everything I needed for the last and final leg was contained within and could I post it back to him when, or rather if, we got there. As he grabbed his bag and said fond farewells to a rather frazzled looking Barbarella I took the moment to have a cursory look through them. I noted we seemed to be missing the one for the entrance to Chesapeake Bay.

"Nothing to worry about", he assured me, "The entrance to Chesapeake is 10 miles wide, just sail in and bang a right. Can't miss it".

Sounded easy enough to me when you put it that way. I then frowned again:

"Didn't you say something about a North Wall or something between here and there?"

"Oh yes, don't worry about that, the Wall is just the term given to when the warm waters of the Gulf Stream coming up the coast meets cold water coming south from Newfoundland and all that. No big issue."

I nodded sagely, having no idea what he was going on about.

We made good progress at first. Then, about 5 days into the trip we encountered what I assumed to be the Wall. The weather deteriorated, dark clouds came studding out of the blue to cover the sky, and soon we were heavily reefed down in a confused and volatile sea. Then came the lightning. Apparently, something about the competing currents and static electricity in the air tends to create the most amazingly violent lightning show in these waters. Barbarella and I looked on helplessly and in terror-stricken awe as strike after strike hit the seas around us. I looked up at the aluminium mast towering above us. Here we were with a great big ruddy lightning conductor drifting around the sea practically screaming out to be hit by a billion volts of electricity.

Now there is much talk in sailing circles about the effects of lightning striking a small boat at sea. Although, as always, there is a great deal of hot air and super-charged opinions it's safe to say not one of the effects described seems to be beneficial to either the boat or indeed those stuck on board. Apparently, the first thing to do, if you do get hit by lightning that is, is to promptly drop dead with cardiac arrest. The positive thing about this is, being dead, you no longer need to concern yourself with all the other effects when a vessel strewn with electronics and sitting on a huge load of water has a billion volts poured through it. If, for some reason you find yourself still alive however, you are then confronted with various scenarios. None of them fun. A fire on board is an obvious option, so too is that everything electrical has been fried including your engine starter motor, GPS, radar, chart plotter and all that other stuff we pretend to understand. It is normally at this stage of the conversation that your salty cove astro-navigator pipes up:

"Well, since I never go to sea without my sextant and my 'ocean ticket', lightning poses no risk to me. I can still find my way by the arcane language of the stars above", he declares sagely pointing vaguely at the bar's smoke-stained ceiling. We all consume this information for a moment until some bright spark points out that you must have an accurate timepiece when using a sextant and unless you have a proper, highly accurate and highly expensive chronometer onboard, your sextant is no use at all, since the electrical watch on your wrist needed to provide 'Greenwich Mean Time or Universal Time Coordinated' or just the right bloody time has also been fried. This leaves us flummoxed until the scientist comes to our rescue:

"What you need", he says wisely, "is a Faraday Cage. You put your GPS, Satellite Phone and other gizmos in the oven or the microwave if you prefer and the lightning simply passes AROUND the items not through them."

This is good science. All we now need, we conclude, is ovens on board big enough to fit you and your crew inside. Try as we might, Barbarella and I couldn't fit into the oven onboard that stormy evening although it did provide us, for a while at least, with an amusing distraction.

Having surprised ourselves by not having been fried alive the previous evening, we arrived, 24 hours later, several miles off the entrance of Chesapeake Bay in the gathering gloom of early evening. Although the GPS was giving an accurate position you could also just follow your nose – you could actually smell the pine trees of Chesapeake miles out at sea. The senses become strangely heightened during long stretches at sea, so I backed up my nose with my eyes by correctly identifying the lighthouse on Cape Henry on the south side of the entrance. Feeling both relieved and pleased with myself I left Barbarella on watch to take us through 'the easy 10 Mile gap and bang a right' as advised. By first light we would be well up and into Chesapeake Bay and near our long-awaited arrival in Deltaville. I went below to get some much earned, in my mind at least, sleep. I was exhausted but looking forward to getting in and enjoying the various delights no doubt awaiting my arrival in world famous Deltaville.

I was woken an hour or so later with Barbarella's huge blue eyes floating only several inches above me. They were bulging slightly more than usual.

"There's some strange lights ahead" she said.

"What kind of lights? Tanker? Fishing boat? Cruise ship?"

"No. Car lights I think.... Thousands of them. Then they disappear into the sea"

I stared at her.

She stared back.

"I'll come up" I said.

The sun had long since gone down and now, emerging on to a blackened deck, I joined Barbarella and we both looked ahead. The sight sent my sleep deprived mind into a bit of a spiral. As far as the eye could see ahead of us there were hundreds of lights spanning the entire huge 10 mile entrance of Chesapeake Bay and these lights were clearly moving fast. I tried to understand what I was looking at. Grabbing the binoculars, I scanned ahead. There WERE trucks and small cars charging along in the darkness and then, mystery of mysteries, seemingly plunging kamikaze-like into the darkness of the sea. A bridge I could understand, but this? If there was an enormous bridge here, had it just collapsed, and we were now dumb witnesses to some horrific unfolding disaster?! Each car plunging to their deaths unable to warn those behind?!

As I stared in confusion Barbarella sensibly dug out the Admiralty sailing instructions for the area. Although lacking any drawings or clear pictures (it assumes the owner isn't a total numpty and has useful things like charts already on board, so it doesn't bother) it did at least mention something called the Chesapeake Bay Bridge Tunnel. This remarkable engineering feat, spanning around 18 miles includes causeways, 4 artificial islands, 2 tunnels, long running trestle bridges and two normal ones, had stood fencing off the entrance of the Chesapeake Bay since the sixties. And I had almost run smack into it. Barbarella helpfully pointed out that, according to the book, there was a way through to the upper reaches of the bay for small boats. It was called the North Channel bridge although she added:

"It may be a bit tight for us".

An hour later, having discovered, almost suicidally, just how 'tight' the North Channel actually was, I finally decided the time had come to make a reasoned decision. We would stop. Right now. Waiting until dawn so we could actually see what the hell was going on we cautiously found a gap where the cars seemingly plunged to their deaths and made our way OVER the Bridge Tunnel with the trucks and other vehicles no doubt merrily hurtling along BENEATH us as we sailed into the Bay. No wonder I was confused.

Tacking back and forth and finally, gloriously, back into chart coverage again we made our way up towards the splendidly named Rappahannock River, turned left at Stingray Point and, as the long, long day drew to a close crept into our final destination, Deltaville marina itself. It had taken almost two months. The beautiful Spanish city of La Coruna was now just a distant memory and here we were, 3725 miles later, in the verdant pine tree surrounded marina of Deltaville in Virginia. We felt the time had finally come to relax, have a beer and rest on our laurels. We motored happily into the centre of the marina looking for an appropriate spot to tie up, hug the nearest tree, rest, relax and get drunk.

Then we ran aground.

MAYDAY

"Can anybody hear me? Is there anybody out there?"

First day out of Marmaris, Turkey and sailing west through the Aegean islands. The sun had been out all day and we were just sitting down to our first supper of the trip. We were all starting to get used to each other and also to the boat, a rather fine Swedish vessel. One of the crew, Ruth, had been labouring for several hours down in the hot galley to procure a fine spread which had just emerged triumphantly from below. Jimmy and I had just started to tuck in. The VHF crackled into life again:
"Can anybody hear me?" A strong Yorkshire accent, a poor distorted signal.

I sighed and looked around. Past the Rhodes channel and into the complex network of Greek islands we had a fresh breeze with all sails out and had made a good start to the voyage back to the UK but now some Englishman had clearly decided to infect the Cyclades with that peculiar English sailor's malaise called the 'Radio Check'.

When approaching the British Isles and wondering where the hell you are, you can ignore your charts and GPS signal and rely instead on the English yachtie's obsession with his VHF radio. You know you're approximately 20 miles off the UK coast when you hear your first 'Radio Check'. As the frequency of said calls increases, you can be pretty certain you're heading towards that great home of English yachting, the Solent. In England, no VHF radio can ever be relied upon to work at any time at all. The only recourse open to the owner is to constantly check the condition of his hardware by calling the Coastguard on the Emergency Channel 16 requesting a 'Radio Check'. In the numerous watering holes of the Solent, it would be deemed scandalously negligent to go to sea and not carry out multiple radio checks as you embark on a journey from, say, Lymington to Yarmouth.

For their part the UK Coastguard has long since given up the ghost of encouraging owners to call the local working channel (like 67 for instance) or call their mate's boat up the river or indeed their wife looking on with concern from the safety of the harbour cafe. No, it is the Great Tradition of English sailors to use the Emergency Channel. No one else anywhere does this. The Coastguard knows, but are rendered powerless to intervene, that someone, somewhere out there is desperately clinging to their upturned hull, clutching their handheld VHF repeatedly screaming 'Mayday! Mayday!' on the Emergency Channel but their genuine calls for assistance have been hopelessly crowded out by a multitude of day sailors having a bun fight over who can get the Coastguard to confirm 'you're loud and clear'. Sometimes I'm sure the Coastguard responds, "your transmission is broken and distorted", just to liven things up a bit.

Anyway, here we were being bothered by a Yorkshireman in the middle of the Greek Cyclades who was clearly suffering with this same odd national affliction. I waited for some other generous soul to comfort the VHF challenged individual. A moment's silence. Nothing. Jimmy looked at me.

"Bloody Yorkshiremen", he said and started piling into his meal. I sighed and pressed the mic on our handheld radio:

"Vessel calling on Channel 16 you're loud and clear. Over".

There was a pause then the VHF crackled again:

"I've sunk me boat and I don't know where I am".

We all stopped eating and looked at each other. Jimmy's sausage actually stopped halfway to his mouth. I picked up the VHF again:

"This is sailing vessel Poppy. You signal is broken and distorted. Can you say again? Over".

"I've sunk me boat and I don't know where I am. Think I'm on a desert island or something. I've managed to scramble up on to this rock here". My heart started pumping harder. I put the handheld down, gave Ruth my uneaten plate and went below to the boat's main, and therefore, far more powerful radio. As I grabbed the mic, the VHF spluttered into life:

"Have I said the wrong thing?"

"This is sailing vessel Poppy. Did you say you've sunk your boat?! Is this a Mayday call?"

"Mayday? Eh yes, I suppose so, I've sunk me boat, Amanda, and I don't know where I am. I were working on me engine and obviously drifted a bit close to this desert island...only had time to grab the radio and a bottle of water before we hit a big rock and down she went like a bloody stone. I did manage to scramble up on this rock though".

The Global Maritime Distress System has precise language and procedures to follow should you hear a distress message. Since I wasn't in distress, although I was quite hungry, there is a call called 'Mayday Relay' which is how you spread the news of a vessel in distress. I tried this one for starters, giving my own name and position. Swiftly and efficiently the Athens based emergency maritime station 'Olympia Radio' responded:

"Poppy, this is Olympia Radio. You make Mayday call?"

"No, I made a Mayday Relay call. I'm fine thank you, but I just picked up a Mayday call from the vessel Amanda whose position is not known".

Answer, "You must give position".

I respond, "but I don't know the position of the casualty".

Olympia Radio: "Then you must find him and save him! We will monitor this channel until you do. Out".

Which brings us to another oddity of the sea. On land, when you see a neighbour's house on fire you naturally call the emergency services and they send a fire engine and professionally trained fire fighters to your neighbour's assistance. They don't generally respond:

"Then you must put out the fire and save your neighbour! Call me back when the fire is out!".

But they tend to at sea.

After a convoluted and rather confusing conversation I managed to extract from 'Dennis', the casualty whom I'd now been instructed to find and save, that he had set sail from Crete a day or so ago and was heading for Marmaris in Turkey. When his engine failed, he had become so engrossed in his efforts fiddling with impellers and crank shafts or whatever, that he hadn't bothered looking around much outside until it was too late. The wind had drifted him into a bay and towards the 'hard stuff'. Realising his plight, Dennis had belatedly decided to get some sails up but whilst he was fiddling with his baggy wrinkling or whatever, the 40 ft vessel had smashed into the rocks surrounding the bay and had begun to break up with surprising rapidity. Dennis, encountering the fast rising water in his saloon, abandoned his attempts at raising the main and had barely enough time to grab his handheld VHF and a bottle of water before leaping heroically onto the nearest large rock, which was now, not surprisingly, pretty close to his vessel. In truth, he probably took a swig of water and stepped onto it.

Scrambling up the side of the desolate, arid Greek island he found himself upon, he had been attempting to signal passing yachts all of whom had happily ignored the obviously sun-crazed Englishman until my voice had finally responded to his increasingly desperate pleas for help. The only trouble was – he, and subsequently I, had no bloody idea where the hell he was.

But we had some clues. The range of a small handheld VHF is pretty limited, and we'd first picked his transmissions up on our own handheld lying in the cockpit tuned, as always, to Channel 16. Since he was also using a handheld and we could actually hear him it was reasonable to assume he was no more than, say, 10 miles away from our position, but we were still sailing at around 6 knots heading roughly west. Were we sailing towards him or away from him? We consulted our detailed charts of the area and concluded there were at least 10 different islands our castaway Yorkshireman could be on. We then looked at his potential route from Crete up towards Marmaris, we knew he had been motoring, so going in a straight line and we knew he'd left a day or so ago. That helped narrow down the options. Dennis had described the island he was on as bleak, rocky, apparently uninhabited and looked 'quite large'. I called him up again, hoping his battery was holding out and that he could still hear us:

"Dennis, this is Robin, we're just trying to locate you. I know your battery is low so keep it simple. Can you describe the bay you're in?"

We waited in silence. Jimmy and I exchanged a worried look. Then the VHF crackled into life:

"Hello Robin, I don't know the name of the place but there's a big bay here, it's all very dry and rocky but I'm alright, I've got me water and I'm just sitting on a rock watching the sun going down. Quite nice actually, if wasn't for sinking me boat and all that."

Another clue and a big one this time, calling on my long years of nautical experience I knew the Sun tended to set, in these parts at least, in the west. So, we were looking for a fair-sized island with a west facing bay somewhere en route from Crete to the Rhodes channel within 10-15 nautical miles of our present position. We consulted the chart again. Jimmy loomed over me and placed an impressively large and rather greasy digit on the western end of an island marked 'Nisos Chalki'. There were four west-facing bays on Chalki island, but I figured we could sail down them all and knock them off one by one. I shouted up the hatch and Jimmy and Ruth altered course to southwest. I double checked everything and called Olympia Radio to give them our guesstimate. Above, I could hear the whining of lines being eased on winches. We were coming round on to the new heading which would take us to the western edge of Chalki. It was a guess but an educated one. The friendly voice from Olympia Radio confirmed they would inform the local police in Chalki who would organise a local boat to rendezvous with us. I hoped to God I was right.

As we picked up speed, all thoughts of dinner long gone and with the sun descending before us I contemplated how relaxed Dennis now sounded during his last transmission. Since all responsibility for his salvation had now been passed onto someone else's shoulders he could now relax and enjoy the view. He had happily started guzzling his only bottle of water and I imagined him perched on his rock, VHF now cast thoughtlessly aside, sitting back and enjoying the beautiful Greek setting sun. He appeared totally unfazed about sinking his own vessel. Perhaps he did this all the time?

I, on the other hand, was now consumed by the fear that I had made the wrong assumptions and we were going, at speed, in totally the wrong direction. What if we don't find him before we lose the light? The nights can be surprisingly cold in the Med. On his own with no rescue in sight and having polished off his only water what would Dennis do next? The batteries on his handheld are surely drained by now, will he attempt to wander inland in search of a road, path, goat track to civilisation? If he IS on Chalki, it is 5 nautical miles across and its only town appeared to be well over on its south-eastern end. Will he attempt the walk during the heat of the day after a night in the open over a dry, rugged and steep landscape? I imagined him scrambling amongst the rocks, falling, breaking his leg, hugging his empty water bottle as he drags himself along some God forsaken desolate Greek valley wailing into his long dead VHF: "Where are you Robin? Why did you abandon me? Why? Why?". I have an active imagination. I worry a lot. I shouldn't really go anywhere near the sea.

An hour later, with the sun set and darkness creeping ominously up on us, we sailed into the first of Chalki's western-most bays. All three of us scanned the bay. Nothing. Jimmy and I exchanged a worried look. In silence we pushed on into the second. Nothing. As we entered the third bay I was standing by with some well-chosen and particularly emotive nautical expletives. Just in case of need. Within moments however Ruth shouted out in triumph:

"I can see the top of a mast. Look!" she added delightedly, "You can just see the sail still set and poking out from the water!" I grabbed the binos and could clearly make out the top metre or so of the mast of a small sailing vessel, the rest of the boat was down having a cup of tea with Davy Jones. We had found the last resting place of the good ship 'Amanda'. Looking further up, perched on the bleak hillside I could also just make out a small, hunched figure looking down on us.

"It that you Robin?" squawked the VHF.

Now we'd found him I could inform my friend in Olympia Radio giving him the exact location of the casualty.

He responded swiftly: "Well done. Now you have to coordinate the rescue. We have lost touch with the boat sent from the only village on Chalki, but it can't be far away from your present position. I hope it's OK".

Jimmy's eyes started to rotate in their sockets. Ruth, who was of a religious persuasion, made a quiet prayer. So, I started to call up the rescue boat on the Emergency Channel. Luckily, they responded pretty quickly, and we could lead them in. We held off the rocks as the shallow bottomed rescue vessel with the local police onboard managed to find a relatively safe spot to retrieve Dennis and his beloved water bottle. Everything else he owned went down with his boat.

Since I was now, it appeared, the designated situation controller, I informed Olympia Radio that the casualty was now safely onboard the rescue vessel which would take him back to Chalki village that evening. It was now dark, and we were keen to get moving again. Olympia Radio was having none of it though:

"You cannot leave. You must accompany the rescue boat back to Chalki. There will be plenty of paperwork to do for you tonight. Ha Ha".

I sighed as we set the sails again and followed Dennis and his new pals around the southern side of the island. It took a while and I couldn't help but ponder how he would have coped with the long walk across the island. Although it was night there appeared, with the total lack of shore lights, to be little to no civilisation outside the charted settlement we were heading to.

The rescue vessel powered ahead of us whilst we pottered along well behind.

Eventually, with midnight approaching, we entered the bay at the eastern end of the island and the welcome lights of the little pretty village illuminated the small marina on one side. Having wasted far too much time fiddling around with our anchor and finally just tying up alongside I made my way to the local police station. Perhaps Dennis would be there, beer in hand, to greet me with an emotional teary-eyed celebration?

"The yacht owner?" the local policeman responded to my query "Oh, he went to bed hours ago."

Fair enough I thought. He hadn't had a good day on the water. After having completed multiple and largely unnecessary witness statements, I bid the police officer goodnight and was pleased to find Jimmy and Ruth relaxing in the last bar open on the front. Jimmy looked at me and silently handed me a beer as I collapsed exhausted on to a spare seat. I looked at my watch, it was now past midnight. We had left Turkey early the previous morning and now here we were, many miles later, on a small island in the Aegean that I'd never heard of before today.

It was the very early hours of the 5th of July. Jimmy gave me his shrewd look.

"Happy Birthday, Skip" he said. I smiled, because it was.

THAT SINKING FEELING

"Jolly nice boat this. And it should be too, for over a million pounds sterling and all that (sorry, don't mean to be vulgar). Strange about all the water in the bilge though. I'm used to dry boats myself".

Boats do have a habit of sinking. Not on me particularly, don't get me wrong I'm not cursed by Poseidon (well, I don't think I am anyway) but it does seem to be a frequent trait that doesn't get much general coverage in the sailing press. I assume this is because if you work in the multibillion pound sailing industry the chances of getting very, very wet indeed aren't something you're going to 'big up' if you're livelihood depends on selling, moving or renovating these remarkably expensive toys. Perhaps the constant opportunity of sinking is part of the appeal? It's seen as a built-in feature of aquatic life that comes free of charge when you set sail. When you've decided to sell up and 'Live the Dream', it's all part of the package, thrown in alongside the free spray hood cover and welcome bottle of Champagne. No doubt the idea is to add some derring-do, a touch of risk, a frisson of icy water, an invigorating brush with Davy Jones's locker and all that to the overall salt strewn experience.

I did a trip once when we had just got going from Gran Canaria in the Canary Islands heading north all the way back to the River Hamble in the UK when, once we heeled over (which tends to happen when you're sailing), we discovered the stern of that particular vessel literally opened up to the seas when its angle changed from the upright. Upon inspection, we discovered the seal between the hull itself and the upper mould (basically the top half of the boat) had delaminated so much that it flexed open when sailing, allowing the blue stuff to pour in. Unsurprisingly, Jimmy and I redirected immediately to the nearest port and again, unsurprisingly, we discovered it was a National Holiday plus the weekend. With no yard open to assist, we were left to puzzle over what to do next. After a bracing cup of tea we pulled off the bumper that runs around the stern of the boat (the 'rubbing strake' it's called) bound the stern to the upper mould with gaffer tape (yes, we stuck the boat together with gaffer tape), shoved the bumper back on and then sealed it all up with Sikaflex (a waterproof sealing compound) for good measure. Upon departure and to everyone's surprise we actually found this worked…until we changed tack that is and the other side opened up… As we sailed frantically towards yet another port of refuge (to gaffer tape up the other side) I'd privately mused upon the call I'd made to the owner the day before, when I'd mentioned his boat appeared to like to sink. He'd replied, "Yes, it does tend to do that. Forgot to mention it…"

Anyway, I digress, the quote at the start of this chapter comes from an eminently likeable owner who had made the puzzled observation that the bilge on his new and highly expensive boat had a strange habit of filling up with water. Being an experienced sailor himself he was used to boats that remained more or less dry down below and now, in the midst of the North Sea, he'd decided to share his disquiet with me. It was about two in the morning.

Several days before, Jimmy and I had flown out to Kiel, jumped into a taxi from the airport and met up with the owners in a small German town called Holtenau on the east end of the rather magnificent 100km long Kiel Canal. A delightful couple, members of the famous Royal Yacht Squadron (or simply 'The Squadron' as it is reverentially known) they religiously put their boat's extra special White Ensign up and down each sunrise and sunset as is the Great Tradition of the Sea ignored by everyone except members of the Royal Yacht Squadron. In explanation of this strange custom, the owner had confided to us in a bare whisper that to NOT do so at the correct time each evening and morning and, horror of horrors, be spotted by another member of the Club would mean...he leant closer, "Losing one's privileges", he said with emphasis.

Jimmy and I silently digested this shocking insight into the upper echelons of British high society, neither fully understanding the metaphor but both impressed, nevertheless. I sensed Jimmy, in particular, was keen to know more (what implement, if any, was used and was it made, perchance, of silver?) but was restrained by his awe of being in the company of such fine examples of the British class system.

For their part and much to their credit (and my amazement) the owners had taken to Jimmy very well.

"Oh, isn't he wonderful! We just love Jimmy", crooned the wife as Jimmy ogle-eyed her slim form from a discreet distance. The owner too, had decided Jimmy was just the type of earthly honest grafter that would be perfect to assist getting the vessel from Kiel back to the UK – the boat's inaugural voyage.

"He's just the sort of chap you'd want next to you in the trenches", he declared. I enthusiastically agreed having always privately thought Jimmy excellent cannon fodder should the need arise – I was just biding my time that's all. Besides Jimmy was very able with a bucket and we needed a bucket that evening.

Having established that we were slowly but remorselessly sinking ("Ah, that would explain the water everywhere", observed the owner) we found ourselves crashing into headwinds on our way to the nearest port of refuge which turned out to be, once I had consulted my Almanac, Ijmuiden in Holland. With Jimmy manfully employing a £5 bucket to save a million-pound boat I now had the opportunity to try to establish which new and exciting place this boat had a hole in. With the boat's state of the art bilge pumps rendered entirely redundant since the yacht builders had forgotten to bore little holes in each segment of the boat to help the water actually get to the bilge area itself, I struggled into the various little holes and crannies looking for the suspect ingress. The steadily rising water was happily filling up the engine area meaning the first thing to go would be the engine although it did at least give us a clue that it was towards the stern of the boat where the problem lay.

Eventually, with all hands helping out with the bucket and many rousing cups of tea, the morning found us motoring, broken but not beaten, into the enormous harbour of Ijmuiden and its equally impressive marina studded with more boat breaking piles than you could shake a stick at. We managed to secure the vessel whilst the owner was having a highly animated discussion with the agent insisting that in his experience selling a boat that had holes in it was really not the done thing at all. We had eventually discovered that the steering rudder itself hadn't been properly sealed – a large gap having been carefully hidden where you couldn't see it, I assume to allow the owner, if he survived, to regale any fellow seafarers he knew, with a heart stopping and suitably dramatic account of his first and perhaps last voyage on his brand new prized possession.

"I shall send a very robust email to the agents", declared the owner, "very robust indeed". Jimmy looked impressed.

"And whilst you are here ensuring the remedial work is completed properly, I insist you make use of the most expensive restaurant in town tonight. I will be happily passing on all costs incurred to the agent so make sure you don't skimp", he said meaningfully. I looked impressed.

That evening, with the boat lifted out of the water and sitting on several sturdy struts, we had explored the local area and eventually tracked down a very pleasant and suitably pricey restaurant within the marina complex itself. I soon found however, that encouraging Jimmy to buy the most expensive steak on the menu proved much harder than getting him to bail out cold salt water with a small bucket for hours on end. Remember Jimmy is not of the South, he is from the Great North, although exactly where is a bit of a mystery.

"Well Jimmy what do you fancy?"

"The steak sounds good but look at the prices Skip – I couldn't possibly, it's daylight bloody robbery it is."

"Have the steak Jimmy."

"I couldn't. Just wrong it is. Just wrong. I'll have the waffles."

"Have the steak Jimmy. Remember we are under orders", I added with emphasis.

"Now the Bordeaux looks good to me. Like to share a bottle?"

"I... it'd be grand having a good red but no way...not at these bloody prices. I couldn't countenance it. I couldn't. Just doesn't feel right that's all."

"Water?" I asked sarcastically.

"£10 for a bottle of water? They must be bloody joking skip".

Sigh.

YANMAR BURGERS

There's no doubt that Cape Town is definitely one of those must-see cities.

Framed by the world-famous Table Mountain, Cape Town has a well-deserved reputation for strikingly clear skies, wonderful geography, friendly locals, an active night life and a fantastic vibrant waterside marina complex called the Victoria and Alfred (known locally as the V & A). Here you could no doubt spend weeks reclining on your yacht's foredeck, ruminating upon a gin and tonic and just taking in the view of the mountain and the bay with the notorious but historic Robben Island just offshore. Our boat, however, wasn't at the V & A. We were down by the old docks and under strict instructions not to, whatever the occasion, walk to the local sailing club at night. "You'd never make it", we were warned, "Far too dangerous." Cape Town, we discovered, was a real mix of beauty and the beast. Overall a terrific place, just watch your back that's all.

Jimmy and I had flown into Cape Town International Airport a couple of days before and had been joined by two young and appallingly keen South African crew for the mammoth journey from Cape Town to the British Virgin Islands around 7000 miles away. Louise, a pretty, slightly eccentric Afrikaner, had spent her first 30 minutes on board dumping her multiple boyfriends in preparation for the trip. Each conversation had lasted about 5 minutes with Jimmy and I trying our best not to listen in too obviously. Well, truth be told, I tried to be discreet; Jimmy just sat opposite her with his eyes bulging and ears revolving like radar to ensure he didn't miss a thing. Having discharged her emotional duties, Louise was now free to enjoy the trip in splendid isolation. Once we got going, she was promptly seasick for 6 days on the trot, a new record in my experience, and spent most of the time staggering around with a small bucket. The bucket was her constant companion, even at dinner time which was a bit disconcerting for the rest of us.

Jimmy privately reckoned Louise's protracted illness was some kind of bizarre nautical revenge perpetrated by her jilted lovers working in cahoots with Poseidon. I thought motion sickness a more likely cause. He looked at me with the patience reserved exclusively for when dealing with people of very little brain.
"No doubt it is Skip.... you know best" he demurred.

The other 'Saffer' as they say was Will, a hardworking and very competent local lad who had jumped on board for the sheer fun of it. Like so many crew he was also toying with the idea of working in the 'industry' and an extra 7000 miles of experience wasn't going to do any damage to his prospects. We also had the benefit of the wisdom of a local sailor who had completed this same run spanning the South Atlantic, I was reliably informed, no less than 13 times. He was on hand to answer our questions, point us in the right direction and generally ensure we didn't blunder aimlessly around getting held up at every street corner. He advised me on the exact amount of propane gas needed for such a lengthy trip and told us where to purchase no less than an impressive 30 Jerry cans to hold our spare diesel. He also told us where to go for a drink when the long day's boat preparation was over.

Long St in downtown Cape Town is actually several streets parallel to each other where sailors, tourists, locals and everyone in between gathers at numerous bars to share stories, swap anecdotes and generally become 'mighty merry' as Samuel Pepys would say. As the evening progressed, it soon became apparent that everyone, everywhere had two very important things to tell us new green necks about life here in South Africa. Firstly, we quickly learnt, there are no less than 11 official languages in South Africa today. People queued up to tell us this. Secondly, everyone was falling over each other to tell us about the last time they were held up at gunpoint. Violence, or the threat of violence, is a very popular topic of conversation. We soon discovered friendly South Africans will merrily exchange blood curdling anecdotes all night if given the chance. Our two local crew also waded in enthusiastically with their own shocking experiences whilst Jimmy and I quietly sipped our beers and kept looking nervously behind our backs. As the evening continued our companions seemed hell bent on out doing each other with their increasingly hair-raising tales of bullets flying through the air and, in defence, flame throwing cars and even, we were confidently told, flame throwing front doors. It made a Saturday night out in Croydon sound really rather quaint.

Having digested all the lessons from the previous night, our boat preparation, inexplicably, sped up somewhat and we were soon ready to depart for the 1st leg; 2000 miles across the mighty South Atlantic to our first stop, the remarkable little British Overseas Territory of St Helena. Sailing out of Cape Town Bay the following sunny morning, dodging vast clumps of kelp, we motored out past Robben Island and were met by a truly enormous pod of dolphins escorting us safely out to sea. There must have been over a hundred of them. I got the impression they'd turned out in force to prove the point that Cape Town is actually a wonderful place and don't get taken in by all the local crime-obsessed gossip. Telling hair-raising tales to foreigners is something South Africans like to do as a kind of harmless national sport. A bit like Australians with all their favourite 'things that can bite you to death' stories. Either way we were off and, with Table Mountain standing proud to our stern, set course for St Helena. We didn't know it then, but we weren't going to St Helena, we were actually on our way to 'Luderitz'. Which is in Namibia apparently.

You get a lot of weather down there at the bottom of the South Atlantic. This is basically because there are two currents circulating in the area: the relatively cold Benguela Current from the west and the much warmer Agulhas Current chugging in from the east. Where they meet, they tend to have a huge bun fight. A couple of days out we found ourselves, and our little boat beneath us, in the middle of this enormous scrap between oceans so we received the usual and inevitable hammering. Having massively reduced the amount of sail on show, Will really took to it however and, as Louise succumbed to the first of her many days of being violently sick, Will dug out some ski goggles (I have no idea why he had ski goggles on board) and seemed to thoroughly enjoy himself at the helm with driving horizontal rain bouncing happily off his visors as he steered us through the violent weather.

Once we had survived the storm, we proceeded upon our way north-westwards towards St Helena. Although the Force 10 winds had been alarming, they had been mercifully short too, and we began to make good progress. That is until Jimmy came up on watch one day and reported that the redoubtable Will was not well. Not well at all. Having discarded his heroic googles to one side, Will had taken to his bunk. Like Louise, he too had been sick but was also heavily fatigued and worst:

"There's traces of blood in his vomit" observed Jimmy.

"I reckon he could be done for Skip, unless we find him a doctor, real quick", he added ominously.

Finding a handy local doctor at sea isn't always easy. It would be nice to think you could simply make a mayday call and a boat full of paramedics would come charging over the horizon in some hugely powerful rib and trundle you off to hospital in no time at all. But they don't. On the whole you're on your own unless you're very near shore indeed. If you have a satellite phone you could always try calling for advice from home. It's possible you may get lucky with the VHF, some passing cruise ship may pick up your distress call and the onboard doctor, bored senseless with geriatric complaints, leaps at the chance to jump into one of the lifeboats and comes over to help you but that doesn't tend to happen very often. No, a far more likely outcome is you'll just have to do the best you can whilst desperately sailing towards the nearest land. Like I said, life on a boat is not like on land but just with blue stuff everywhere, it comes with strings attached. And sometimes those strings will pull you in an unexpected direction.

I didn't know anything about Namibia other than it has two ports, Walvis Bay to the north and further south a little place no one's heard of called Luderitz. Having checked Will's pulse, inspected his vomit, and shone a torch into his eyes to check the size of his retina (we did that bit for fun) Jimmy and I declared Will should now be known simply as 'the casualty'. He seemed relieved by this and asked if this meant he could skip his watches. Considering that Jimmy secretly thought he wouldn't make it at all, we decided to let him off for now and gave him leave to stay in bed. As Jimmy went off to search the boat, he told me, for a suitably sized body bag I consulted our charts of the South Atlantic and drew a line to the nearest port from our position. The line ended at 'Luderitz'. I didn't have a detailed chart for Luderitz. We went there anyway. What choice did we have?

Thus, it was, that seven days out from Cape Town we found ourselves feeling our way in to a new and mysterious port on the west coast of Africa on a cold and misty dawn. Emerging rather dramatically out of the early morning gloom some very large Namibian fishing vessels inadvertently showed us the way in but we proceeded cautiously nevertheless – letting the sun burn the moisture away to reveal our route into the bay and ultimately the small reception pontoon that my South Atlantic pilot book mentioned briefly in its description of the old German port. I used the VHF to inform the authorities we had a very sick crew aboard. They didn't seem too concerned but helpfully let us tie up briefly on the dinghy dock to unload Will who was assisted off to the local European run clinic as we cleared in with the friendly Customs guy who had also talked us in on radio.

Having safely moved our vessel on to a mooring buoy in the harbour and with both crew now gently convalescing, one on board having finally decided to stop being seasick, the other being well attended to in the local clinic, Jimmy announced it was now time to explore the town of Luderitz. Five minutes later we were sitting down reviewing the menu at 'Barrels' restaurant and bar – a charmingly atmospheric watering hole near the marina that felt like it'd been there for ever. Perched on one of their tall stools round little round tables and surrounded by subtle little lights and ancient barrels (hence the name) Jimmy expressed that in his opinion at least the trip had started "very well" and he was already looking forward to the next leg, the 1500 miles to St Helena. I stared at him blankly then remembered my manners:

"Oh well... yes, I suppose so. Shame about Will chucking up blood and at death's door and then poor Louise just chucking up everywhere, of course. She really has become much attached to that little bucket of hers...Bit off course at the moment too but can't be helped, I guess. Let's hope they both recover soon, eh."

A pause whilst Jimmy looked around him contentedly. An elderly lady, clearly the worst for wear herself, gracefully slid off the stool behind him and crashed to the floor. Her equally drunk companions looked down upon her sympathetically as she lay at their feet. Nobody moved.

"Another beer Jimmy?" I ventured.

"Don't mind if I do Skip, don't mind if I do", he said happily.

We spent four days in Luderitz. Jimmy declared he would go off exploring the diamond mine fields nearby to see "if something turns up" as he put it. Will, being carefully nursed by an increasingly attentive Louise, made a startlingly swift recovery. Louise, having initially looked like calling it a day herself now gamely declared she, too, would soldier on. Will's recovery had nothing to do with this apparently. After a couple of days absence Jimmy suddenly emerged back on board in some haste. He had wandered, as he had said he would, into the famous diamond fields of the area and something had actually turned up - a man with a large gun. The days of strolling around picking up diamonds just lying around were obviously over it appeared and Jimmy and crew were now ready to move on. With some regret we said our farewells to 'Barrels' and headed once more out to sea. Then the fog descended upon us. And we didn't have radar.

Now there's one thing I really hate about working on sailing boats, one thing that really gets my goat and has me nervously twiddling with my life jacket toggle each time and generally wishing I were more religious. That one thing is being stuck in thick fog without radar. Now, I know that in addition to radar there's also a very useful thing called Automatic Identification System (AIS) which shows you the speed and position of other boats around you on your handy chart plotter. It's a great bit of kit. But we didn't have that too. Like ours not all boats have AIS on board so those that don't are therefore invisible. Radar doesn't miss them though. Radar, if you have it tuned correctly, picks up everything out there. Without it in heavy fog you're blind. Being blind and not knowing whether your watch will suddenly come to a watery end, when the last thing you see is a huge bow come steaming out of the gloom on top of you, is not a nice experience. I had a crewmember once who, in heavy fog, decided to simply dig out a good book and read the watch away oblivious to the risks attached. Coming up on deck and upon confronting him, he merely pointed out in his defence:

"Well, I can't see anything with all this fog everywhere so thought I'd just have a good read instead".

I'd been asleep in my bunk during his watch for several hours. Gets me jumpy even thinking about it.

The fog lasted a long time. Well, it felt like it anyway. Eventually and after much nail biting on my part, we emerged mercifully unscathed and continued on our way to St Helena. Perhaps to calm Will's nerves and no doubt as an integral part of his convalescence, Louise had now moved into the same cabin with Will. Jimmy hadn't noticed though.

St Helena. Dawn. After 10 days, we found ourselves drifting off the north coast of this dramatic and incredibly isolated British island, waiting for the sun to come up so we could motor into the relatively protected bay. There's no marina there, of course, and there was only one other boat, a small little vessel with a retired chap on board who had been roaming the high seas alone for far too long. He was, therefore, a proper sailor with a great big beard, rough hands and skinny little legs who looked at our catamaran with barely concealed distaste.

"Don't anchor too close to me", was his advice so I didn't, crowded anchorage and all that. He'd left the rat race to get away from it all and here he was, in the middle of nowhere having to fight off yet another boat – with us that made two boats in the anchorage. St Helena was no better than London in his opinion. I told him I quite liked London. That confirmed all his worst fears.

Awaiting the boat ferry, we tuned into the local radio, Radio St Helena. It was in the midst of playing the Laughing Policeman and, as that memorable hit from the 1920s faded away, we listened intently to the News. Apparently, St Helena was in the midst of political elections fever and the various hustings had commenced around the island. One such gathering reported a disappointing turn out however, just three people including, I assume, the competing candidates, had emerged. Perhaps the three also included the breathless reporter from St Helena radio but we couldn't quite make it out before the young and enthusiastic DJ launched into the other latest breaking news. Someone apparently had a cow to sell and another St Helena resident was also trying to find a home for a 12v car battery. We were all given his number live on radio. Jimmy frantically grabbed a pen and paper but, too late, the moment was gone. No wonder our reluctant companion across the water was so enraged by our presence, this place couldn't handle any more action.

St Helena really is a remarkable place. An island lost in time, well about 1820 anyway, so we took the opportunity to squeeze in a tour round the island on a jeep and witnessed the beginnings of the construction of the new airport which will no doubt open the place up a bit, perhaps to the 20th century if not the 21st. If you find yourself in St Helena with time to kill, there are several points of interest that you will feel compelled to experience: climbing up the quite ludicrously steep Jacob's Ladder in the capital Jamestown is one of them. After 200 steps, you will consider this very good exercise and a good workout for the heart. Halfway up the 699 steps, you will regret ever considering it good for you, after 500, you will regret being born. No one has ever made it to the top alive.

St Helena's other biggest claim to fame is that it is pretty much in the middle of nowhere and thus provided a suitably isolated spot to lock up the world's most dangerous Frenchman, Napoleon Bonaparte. This was in 1815, which was the last time anything really happened on St Helena. The British authorities had already tried to do the same in Elba in the Mediterranean, but it didn't, shall we say simply, 'work out'. In St Helena you can visit his rather grand house, Longwood, and his tomb. Both properties are now vacant, Bonaparte's body having been removed by the French long ago after a lengthy and protracted argument about the wording on the tomb itself. Apparently, the French wanted to take the opportunity of singing his eternal glories with a carefully worded eulogy of the man's many, many remarkable achievements. The British for some reason didn't feel quite the same way about him. So, they left it blank instead. I guess Napoleon was passed caring by that point too.

As part of his recuperation, Will dispatched himself off to the impressively large local hospital for a check-up after his recent illness. He proudly took his blood test results from Luderitz with him. Apparently, the British doctor took one look at them and exclaimed, "And they let you leave? With these figures?!"

That evening we marked our imminent departure from this quite beautiful island by dining out in style at the only restaurant on the island, Anne's Place, owned unsurprisingly, by Anne. We reserved a table just to make sure we beat the rush and asked for a copy of the menu. There is no menu at Anne's Place – you don't need one. Just turn up and eat whatever they serve you. It's all good though. Having signed and left our mandatory flag at the restaurant, as is the Great Tradition, we jumped on the boat ferry and got on our way. As Jimmy and Will raised the mainsail I waved merrily at our friend in the anchorage as we departed. He looked back at me with that 'one born every minute' expression that I have been trying to perfect ever since. At least he could get some peace and quiet now.

Before us lay the long haul to the Caribbean. Four thousand miles of ocean with not a lot in between but at least we had the Southeast Trade Winds behind us, and a big fat sail called a gennaker set up forward. Although it was a knackered old thing described by the owner as a 'sacrificial sail', it heroically did us proud and we made good progress. Skirting round Ascension Island, which looked even quieter than St

Helena, we pushed on into the depths of the South Atlantic charging up towards the Equator. Where it all fell apart.

I run a dry boat. Which means no alcohol on board. Crossing the Equator however, I admit, is a major salty sea dog event, so I had let all on board have one token beer each to celebrate the momentous occasion. I know, sounds 'Bah Humbug', but boats and alcohol don't mix. Believe me on this one. I must confess we also didn't bother dressing up and prancing around pretending to be Poseidon either, because it is a rather silly thing to do. One tradition we did adhere to though, was to pour a small libation to the gods to thank them for our deliverance thus far. I privately noted Louise forgot to do this. The next day the wind died. The day after that we ran out of gas. Then we experienced a biblical plague...which was just weird.

Running out of wind is a pain but I had at least brought along a vast quantity of spare diesel in Jerry cans to keep the boat moving in such an event. The helpful guys at the fuel dock in Cape Town had taken it upon themselves to secure the cans lids with a tightening tool which I thought a good idea at the time since the last thing you want is spilled diesel rolling around your bilges. A good idea that is until we needed the fuel. Having struggled with opening the damn super-tightened lids and made use of every nautical expletive I know and still made no headway; I was left wondering just how messy it was going to get when I took an axe to the cans. Will and Louise also gamefully had a go, but they just wouldn't budge. Jimmy looked on benignly waiting until we had exhausted ourselves, strolled over, and made good use of his remarkably large hands. The diabolical Jerry cans, recognising their fate, immediately surrendered. We all agreed our previous efforts, however, must have loosened them.

Running out of gas is not so easily resolved, however. I glumly reflected back to the words of our 'local expert' in Cape Town, who had told me confidently I had bought more than enough propane for the trip – perhaps all the lovely cakes Louise had baked weren't such a good idea now? Either way the buck stops with the Skipper. I had messed up big time. Sensing my disappointment Jimmy, 1st Mate and the 'kind of man you want with you in the trenches' rose to the occasion. He expressed his determination to resolve our lack of cooking gas problem using 'cunning mechanical, electrical and even chemical solutions' to ensure we had piping hot meals every evening.

"Don't you worry yourself, Skip – I'll sort this out. No problem". Louise and Will looked impressed. I just looked worried.

The next day Jimmy's great salvational culinary experiments began. To my, and possibly Jimmy's, surprise they actually began quite well. He started with a large can of tuna. Emptying the contents out and cleaning it whilst not completely removing the lid meant you could fill the can with methylated spirits, close the lid, light the edge and hey presto create a small camping stove. This actually worked pretty well until we ran out of white spirit. Jimmy then began to focus his newfound energy on the engine. Now, as I said, the wind had died, so we were motoring...a lot. We used up every drop of spare fuel to keep the boat going during a 10-day wind drought. Motoring on one engine only (very wasteful to use both at once) and at low revs to conserve our fuel stockpile, the Yanmar engines were on day and night as we switched between the two of them. Diesel engines on boats tend to run at a temperature of about 80-85°C. That isn't very hot but can at least provide the elements of a slow cooker. Jimmy began with eggs like they did in all those 2nd World War films. It didn't work and just made a terrible mess. He then tried to boil pasta in a pan attached to the engine. The subsequent floury gloop was quite frankly inedible and, despite our best efforts to humour Jimmy, Will decided it might bring on a relapse, so we ditched it.

Jimmy then moved on to using the engines to cook meat; now this was much more successful. Wrapping minced meat up in foil, after adding some spices for fun and then double wrapping it all up again to stop all those meat juices spoiling the engine actually produced something approaching a slow cooked burger. Having carefully left his silvery packages lying on top of the engine, turning occasionally for a nice consistent finish, Jimmy had triumphantly produced what he declared were 'the finest Yanmar burgers in the land'. The only problem was it took 8 hours (at 1600rpm if you're interested in recreating this culinary experiment, although God knows why you'd try). By the time the Yanmar burgers were ready to eat it was about midnight – still it was without doubt one of my most memorable feasts on board.

The problem with the glorious triumph of the Yanmar burgers was that it gave Jimmy a great deal of exaggerated confidence in his own abilities. Fly too close to the sun and you'll get burnt. The vessel we were sailing had, for some reason, various bottles of cleaning and scrubbing chemicals on board including the aforementioned white spirit, acetone and other dodgy nautical chemical solutions. Jimmy now turned his inexorable attention to these bottles as sources of flame and heat.

In the covered area to the stern of the vessel Jimmy started to construct a pop-up lab. Having carefully laid out a protective surface Jimmy started to mix, in small doses at first, then in alarmingly increasing amounts highly noxious and flammable concoctions that he assured me he had 'thoroughly tested in controlled conditions'. Once he had discovered the right mix, he assured me, we would have an inexhaustible supply of fresh clean fuel that we could use on top of the oven in the galley.

While he was beavering away in his newly created mad scientist lab, the rest of us kept our distance and continued to dine each evening on cold tomatoes and beans. After a day or so of feverish activity Jimmy announced he had discovered the perfect mix, both flammable and non-exploding, and had made a sizeable pot of it on the galley top. He confided in me that he was even thinking of privately marketing it as a new type of 'clean cooking fuel'. With a flourish he lit the solution.

I can still see now, in my mind's eye, Jimmy's look of bewildered confusion as the resulting chaos spread. Emanating from his prized little cauldron, the flames simply erupted. Darts of fuel crazed missiles came spurting out of the centre and began showering the stove top. They reminded me of little fireworks as they happily flew around the galley. As the show got into its rhythm Jimmy stood dumbfounded and motionless, perhaps dazed by his own brilliance, or more likely appalled by what he had just created. The show did at least provide the rest of us with an opportunity to practice our fire-fighting skills. As Jimmy stared on, zombie-like, Will and I quickly put the fire out and Louise helped us clean the galley down. Miraculously nothing had been damaged, other than Jimmy's pride that is. Later, as we sat down to cold soup which now tasted just fine to us, we watched Jimmy sullenly packing away his pop-up lab. He was strangely pensive for a couple of days. Then the wind came back. And things started turning really quite surreal.

It blew in with a vengeance. Howling out of the night we went from sailing along just fine to desperately reefing down the sails and grumbling generally about 'feast or famine'. We were now some 200 miles off the coast of French Guyana and finally making decent progress towards Barbados some 600 miles away. Having made the boat safe, I crashed out leaving Jimmy on watch. The following morning, I woke up, for once, without someone shaking me awake in a panic and made my way into the saloon. The sun had been up for a while now, so I was surprised to see the saloon doors locked shut. The weather had moderated and we appeared to be making comfortable speed. I flicked through the logbook, the hourly record of all and sundry that we maintained with religious zeal on the hour every hour. Will was now on watch and he'd written something unusual in the 'comments' section:

'Boat covered in insects and dragonflies' was the terse description. I frowned and opened the doors to go outside.

Going up the short curvy steps to the cockpit area I found Will sitting wrapped up by the helm with the autopilot ticking over. From behind his hood he gestured to me, but I was too busy taking in and trying to process what I was seeing.

The boat was covered by a biblical plague of dragonflies. There were simply thousands of them. Having reeled briefly at this bizarre turn of events, I now looked closer and discerned two distinct types had arrived, one red and one green, each measuring around 6cm long and they seem to have decided, overnight, to turn our boat into one huge floating colony. They were everywhere, burrowing their little heads into the mesh that protected the windows, battling to sit on all the lines, getting stuck in the cockpit hatches whilst others were happily buzzing around our heads and bashing themselves senseless on the sails. Even more remarkable was a small gathering of some kind of small tropical wood bug, these little brown guys had formed a breakaway group by the helm and were busy either eating or mating with each other, we couldn't quite be sure. Will watched them, clearly fascinated. He explained that all the windows and doors were sealed shut to stop our new shipmates getting into our bunks last night.

After a lengthy discussion of how far dragonflies can fly (remember we were at least 200 miles from the nearest shore) we agreed they must have been blown out to sea by the recent heavy weather and then drawn collectively towards our ship's lights during the night. They must have come from miles around to join the party. Maybe Jimmy's fireworks had helped? At that point Jimmy himself emerged from his pit and silently joined us sitting together in the cockpit. He looked around himself slowly, whilst nonchalantly flicking off a red dragonfly that had landed on his left leg.
"You do attract some strange folk, Skip, I'll give you that." he said.

A week later and having cleared away the corpses of thousands of tropical insects we were there at last, the British Virgin Islands, the jewel in the crown of yachty heaven under a steaming sun-drenched Caribbean sky. These are the places that parade themselves over every sailing magazine cover everywhere in the world and are therefore responsible for many a boat owner's broken dreams and subsequent reduction to (relative) poverty. Having crept through Round Rock Passage in the dead of night with not a soul in sight, we cruised gently up the Drake Channel towards Tortola, the biggest island in the multi-island chain. On arrival at any new country, it's obviously important and necessary to 'clear in' with the authorities ashore where customs forms and immigration officials check through your passports, boat documentation and generally ensure you're not bringing anything or anybody untoward into their country. Since we were no longer a drifting insect colony, I had high hopes things would proceed smoothly.

The best advice to give concerning clearing in anywhere in the world is dress relatively neatly, smile serenely and comply as best as you possibly can with all bureaucratic procedures however daft they may seem. This approach tends to work fairly well wherever you end up. Not in Road Town, Tortola, however. I have arrived in Tortola on many different boats and have tried to follow the procedures as best I can each time. Learning from my mistakes, I have altered my approach on each occasion, with the only result being that whatever approach I took, it was always the wrong one. For instance, I have tried sailing alongside the official customs pontoon only to be told that I should have called up first and that this pontoon was for 'different boats' anyway. I have anchored off as instructed and called up the authorities to request clearance on VHF only to be ignored forever. I'd still be there today if I hadn't given up and reported into the nearest marina only to be told I'd done the wrong thing again. On my third attempt and having once more been heavily berated for 'not following official procedures', I remember asking politely what were the correct procedures? This request was met with stony silence.

Recounting these tales of woe prior to our arrival I detected a certain level of incredulity stemming from Jimmy and Co., so I took them along this time for the ride. Jimmy sat mutely looking on as I was informed that our passports would be confiscated because we hadn't turned up with pre-booked outgoing flights (we had arrived that morning and gone straight to the authorities) and, once we had booked flights, were asked petulantly why they were in two days' time and not tomorrow? I resisted the temptation to remind them that since we were delivering yachts to the 'BVI' for the sailing industry, we were actually a small but rather important part of the tourist economy, a large part of which is people sailing around the islands on charter holidays. Which would have been an entirely futile comment and would no doubt have led to us all been thrown into the nearest prison on the grounds that, I assume, we knew too much. After many more attempts I have now cracked the mystery and know exactly what to do when checking into Tortola. Go to Virgin Gorda and check in there instead.

There is one advantage however that our long-suffering customs and immigration friends have in Road Town. Diagonally opposite the red roofed building is another old sailors' watering hole, Pusser's Pub of Pusser's Rum fame. Having successfully retrieved their passports and calling their fond farewells behind them, Louise and Will had already skipped off merrily into the sunset together. The boat, lying safe and sound in a nearby marina, had been thoroughly cleaned in and out and was now awaiting its first charter guests blissfully unaware of the trials and tribulations that had got it there. Having successfully been granted 'legal-for-now' status Jimmy and I wandered into the dark interior of Pussers. Things had changed somewhat from my first experience of the bar, when there were twenty plus riotous Astrid-smocked trainees shouting and laughing whilst demanding service. The place had refocussed quite sensibly on to the sizeable cruise ship market and had restyled itself more as a themed sailing restaurant than the real boozy sailors bar of the past. One thing hadn't changed though. I requested a couple of large, tinned mugs of 'Painkiller', a local rum sodden cocktail which comes in various strengths dependent upon your level of need – we ordered two 'Admirals' which took about a bottle of the stuff to fill them.

Jimmy sighed contentedly as we reclined at the bar watching our drinks taking form. Plenty of ice we noted but plenty of rum too. The heat of the day was easing off, the fans whirled overhead. The room lit by multi-coloured window tiles taking the heat out of the Caribbean sun and filtering splashes of red, blue and green gently throughout the interior. Jimmy rested his massive hands on the bar and looked around him at the quasi authentic Royal Navy themes surrounding us. Stern faced matelots stared down on us from the past whilst a lost American tourist asked the way to the authentic salty sailor gift shop out the back. As I sat there looking out across the bay I observed an enormous cruise ship slowly manoeuvring its ludicrous bulk out to sea, looking at it made me feel my work and all our efforts were like a dinosaur from another age. A token of the past adrift in the present. The 'Admirals' arrived. Jimmy removed the pink little umbrella in his drink with distaste before he sampled his massive Painkiller. His eyes lit up as the local rum made its presence felt. He looked up again at the cracked black and white images of sailors long since passed away. Their cool capable looks seemed to mock us across the years.

'You think you've had it tough, do you?' they seemed to say.

Jimmy caught my eye and looked up at the faded photograph, "Times change Skipper", he declared suddenly and then looked at me with his shrewd look, "But people don't".

I smiled and we quietly toasted each other and took a long swig. Some distantly remembered lines of F Scott Fitzgerald came to me:

"And so, we beat on, boats against the current, drawn back ceaselessly into the past".

Jimmy sighed contentedly.

"Sometimes, Skipper, you can be a real twat you know" he said.

BOB THE BUILDER

The owner's name was Bob. And he was a builder.

A very tough Northern uncompromising builder with a large, pleasant brother, Geoff, who must have weighed in at 18 stone. Bob had bought an impressive new French yacht to 'make some money out of it' and needed a helping hand to get it across the Med in one piece. The idea that anyone could buy a yacht and make some sort of profit on it was a new and surprising concept for me. Just contemplating buying a yacht indicates a triumph of optimism over reality in itself, the idea that you could actually make money out of the remarkably expensive things was new and exciting information. Also, along for the ride was John, Bob's joiner mate who, at a loose end since his employer had suddenly grown an interest in sailing, had been offered a post on this trip – as crew. The fact that John had never got on board a boat before in his life was not considered an impediment, in fact it was considered a plus – unsullied by knowledge John could prove to be an instinctive sailor learning from the keel up as they say. Bob however told me he had 30,000 sea miles under his belt but strangely none of these miles included any night-time sailing although Geoff did have some night miles since he'd 'crossed the channel once' but hadn't done much else. Which was why I was there, I guess.

Several weeks before Bob had made himself abundantly clear to the office:
"I can sail well enough myself but I'll need someone to help me out a bit with the new boat and that but" he added ominously "if you send me a bloody pedantic RYA wanker we'll friggin' eat him".
So, they sent me.
I wasn't sure how to take this but decided it was a sign of my growing maturity rather than my expendability. With four of us on board, alas there was no room for Jimmy on this trip, a fact he took rather well. Perhaps too well. It was Mistral time in the Med, a particularly nasty localised wind and our departure took

us straight into and across the Gulf de Lyon, the epicentre for the Mistral. A point lost on the owner but not on Jimmy. Besides, he said, he had some 'unfinished business' to attend to apparently, which sounded like a quickly invented excuse to me but since he gave no more information, I left it at that.

Crossing the Mediterranean by yacht sounds like a delightful and exotic past-time and it no doubt can be if you do it the sensible way: short hops, following the coast, taking it easy, pulling in whenever you want or like or before sunset or when you're short on beer and all that. With the owner and his friends on board, I was looking forward to a novel experience, actually being on a boat going slowly and smoothly from one sun speckled marina to the next with haughty dinners ashore and much heart cheeringly invented sailing anecdotes from all as we sunk sundowners well after the sun itself had gone to bed. As the drinks went down, I imagined our stories becoming ever more farcical, with fine lines like:
"So, I said to him 'blow me if that's a Force 10 pass the gin and tonic old chap and we'll get the No 1 spinny out' ha ha ha". This sounds even better if you're wearing bright red trousers. Like

every serious sailor we always do our best sailing in the bar. We have to. It's the law.

Bob had other ideas though: "I know the boat's got some issues and we're not ready, but I want to get cracking. We need to get to Turkey ASA bloody P to get this boat paying its wages. Can't believe how much I've had to shell out for the damn thing already," he fumed.

"But the Mistral is blowing", I tentatively pointed out and showed them the weather forecast. It had lots of big arrows on it and dark colours, which isn't generally a good sign unless you actually want to go for a very cold swim miles from land.

"It would be suicide to leave now. Perhaps we could get these issues sorted whilst we're here in the yard because as soon as we leave, that'll be it. We'll be out of sight, out of mind and we'll have to pay for the work elsewhere. Here it's free."

Bob contemplated this.

The weather thing was obviously because I was a soft-as-shite Southerner but the mention of money may have swung the balance since, for once, reason prevailed and we held up for a couple of days giving the yard time to finish the work. It was a brand-new boat for starters, which meant it had loads of problems that needed solving.

Which brings me to another Great Tradition of the Sea. When you buy a new car you kind of expect it to work, go forward and backwards and not blow up, that kind of thing. Not with a yacht. There are always problems. This is partially due to the complexity of modern sailing yachts and partially due to the fact that each yacht is a relatively unique experiment in making a thing that floats most of the time. When you buy a new 'mid-range' car for instance it may be production model number 251,784. When you buy a yacht it may well be hull number 7 (if it's a popular model) and that includes the hulls used in boat shows and effectively all previous research and development hulls. The result is something that has to happily exist in a highly hostile environment with virtually no test models and since there's always tweaks and changes for the owner (who promptly loads 2 ton of his own gear all over the boat) each yacht is unique. No wonder there are always 'teething problems' - every day's a new and exciting journey into the unknown. Throw in suicidally optimistic owners and hapless crew and it's remarkable things work out at all but most of the time they do. Well, most of the time anyway.

When we finally departed the strong winds had blown themselves out and we had a nice gentle light breeze to allow all on board to get used to the boat and the watch system. Now we'd left our recent home of Guissan, Bob, hot foot from being dead keen on charging headfirst into the Mistral, immediately started chucking up, soon accompanied by Joiner John. Eighteen stone Geoff, for his part, seemed fine. As for me I was just relieved that anyone on board was actually listening to me. We made our way south-southeast heading for the rather infamous Straits of Bonafacio. This narrow channel that divides Corsica and Sardinia tends to create a funnelling effect with the wind, so it can be nice and mild on either side and blowing a hoolie in the middle. Sadly the US and UK Maritime Coastguard Agency and indeed the Royal Yachting Association themselves don't recognise the term 'hoolie' and can't agree amongst themselves whether to spell it 'hooley' or 'hoolie' but it's one of those terms that non-mariners understand immediately. It means stay at home.

For once, however, the Straits of Bonfacio were in benign mood and we briefly popped into Bonafacio itself to pick up fuel. A beautiful colourful town perched around the marina, it would have been great to tarry a while, but we were on Bob's tight schedule and ploughed on. As we departed Joiner John announced, not for the first time, that he was unhappy and pointed out that now he'd been onboard a sailing yacht for a couple of days he had no doubt that he now possessed all the necessary experience to stand his own watch without any company or assistance.

This brings me to yet another strange rule of the sea – the less experience you have of sailing, the more confident you are of your own nautical abilities. As your experience grows, however, and more 'interesting things' happen, the less you are confident. Indeed, my great hope is to one day be so experienced that I will be too terrified to ever step foot on a boat again. Only then will I know I have become a proper Master Mariner and can feel sufficiently qualified to prop up bars in maritime pubs around the world insisting on providing entirely gratuitous advice to all within barking distance. These old boys, they do tend to be men of a certain age, are the last true heroic sailors of our and the next generation and are my favourite people in sailing bars.

One memorably wine sodden French salty cove once publicly derided me from sheltering 'like a little girl' from a gale in the small but perfectly formed bolthole, Camaret, near Brest in France whilst the wind howled manically outside the safety of the inevitable 'Irish' bar we had found there. My crew and I smiled on indulgently over our Guinness's as he reminded us all, whilst pumping his chest, that 'We are the Master of the Seas' and shouldn't worry about weather forecasts, storms and 10 metre waves. We were so impressed with his undoubted wisdom on the subject that we bought him another drink and encouraged him to tell us more. He's probably still there now cornering some poor visiting Englishmen too timid to take his 30-footer out into gale force winds on a coast with more lighthouses than streetlights.

But even our heroic French friend was nothing compared to the salt-stained and heavily imbibed Englishman who berated me and crew for timidly sailing our boat through the Kiel Canal from the Baltic to the Dutch / German coast and thereby avoiding much of the oil rig-laden and violently ill-disposed North Sea. We were at that stage holed up in a bar in Cuxhaven on the Elbe awaiting a weather window to progress in to 'Riddle of the Sands' territory to the west on the way to the UK. Impressed by his obvious knowledge on the subject I asked him whether he had ever sailed through the North Sea himself.

"You're joking, aren't you? Oh no, of course not", he admonished me, "but a mate of mine did once a couple of years back and, you know what?", we all leaned in expectantly, "He told me it was REALLY rough!"

Joiner John had, no doubt, been influenced by learned fellows like our brave Frenchman and heroic drunken Englishman and I was therefore encouraged to adapt the watch system accordingly. Which I promised I would do as soon as the opportunity arrived, like when we got to our final destination for instance.

As we sailed onwards southeast past the volcanic and very striking Aeolian islands with some still smouldering dramatically, the next funnelling effect occurs between Sicily and Italy itself in the infamous Straits of Messina. This funnelling however is different, not wind this time but a concentration of ferries. As we approached, I briefly wondered what the collective noun for ferries is; a 'Messina' fits pretty well. Since there is still no bridge linking Sicily to the Italian mainland a remarkable number of ferries ply their trade across these narrow, heavily congested waters. Homer spoke (or recited if you are a damn pedantic classicist) of the ancient whirlpool Charybdis on one side and the monster Scylla on the other.

These ancient horrors have been replaced (although Charybdis is still honoured by particularly nasty overfalls here) by the very modern horrors of massive Roll-on Roll-off ferries that come hurtling out at you at breakneck speeds as you creep up or down the channel dodging the big cargo vessels and tankers that still use the Messina straits as part of their routing to or from the Eastern Mediterranean. These ferries come in all shapes and sizes but seem to have one thing in common. The ferry skippers are clearly so bored of going back and forth all day and all night, the only distraction left to them is in terrorising little sailing boats. I'm not suggesting, of course, that they're deliberately trying to run you down but are simply having a bit of fun seeing how close they can get to you before letting you live another day. They probably like yachts. We're the only thing that keeps them sane I suppose.

Events on board Bob the Builder's boat were becoming slightly less sane themselves as we dodged our way past the Straits expecting to be crushed at any moment, crept past Reggio de Calabria with the foulest marina water in the Med and made our way down towards the southern side of the Peloponnese. Joiner John, caught between vomiting and defecating in the forward heads, had decided to take the middle route between these extremes by smashing his considerably tough head through the solid shower screen. Staggering out holding his head in one hand and the large, shattered remnants of the screen in the other he wailed that, "Bob was fockin' going to kill me", before retreating to pull his trousers up and continue with the main event of 'feeding the fishes', as Frank would say.

Not to be outdone, the next day Geoff also lurched his impressive bulk into the one remaining solid shower screen in the aft loos and emerged equally appalled at the carnage he had committed, waving the large shards above his head as Bob berated him for being a "fockin' clumsy bastard".

In the confused sea state that is so often the norm in the Med, John also struggled with the joys of cooking afloat. As the watch system always incorporates 'galley duty' we all have to take our turn at preparing lunch or cooking up a dinner of sorts which means Joiner John had to do his fair share too. And he wasn't happy about it. Not happy at all.

And I for one don't blame him. I have great sympathy for ships' cooks. There should be a charity for them. It doesn't matter how much sailing you do and how many nautical miles have passed beneath your keel. I don't care if you've been 'born on a boat' and come from a great line of sailors descended from Captain Cook or the captain of the Titanic or something. The naked truth, cunningly hidden by every yachting agent and sailing guru, is cooking on board a boat at sea is a right royal pain in the backside. Of course, it all looks fine and dandy on a boat in a marina or at a boat show. Modern galleys are expansive, clean and bright with Corian work surfaces and acres of cupboards, microwave ovens, fridge freezers and even dishwashers. No doubt some bright spark will come up with granite surfaces soon giving naval architects some interesting challenges concerning arcane problems like boat 'list' and 'loll'. Wandering on board a brand-new galley at the boat show is like stepping into a New York apartment over-looking Central Park. What could be simpler? It's just like at home just better and neater. Don't be fooled. Remember the galley isn't moving wildly around because it's in a marina or elevated on stilts at the boat show. At sea it is, and it makes preparing and cooking food remarkably dangerous. Yes, we all have to do it but it's an activity you endure not enjoy. If you doubt this and lacking a boat on which to test my theory, there is an alternative. Luckily, you can replicate the experience of cooking at sea without ever stepping off dry land.

Indeed, you don't even need to leave the house. You can just use your own kitchen at home but will need to make some simple alterations prior to knocking up your first proper nautical dinner this evening (remember we normally cook for 3 or 4 people on board). The first step and before any marine cooking takes place is cover the kitchen floor with some highly slippery surface, some top kitchen floor cleaning brands will do. Then get yourself into a pair of roller skates, the less familiar you are with these the better. Next get your wife/husband/friend to tie a rope around your waist and get them to stand well back holding the rope. Pick out your largest sharpest knife and attempt to stand in the middle of the kitchen in front of a large chopping board whilst your kids, standing a safe distance away roll the potatoes, onions, carrots, meat of choice and so on back and forth between themselves with you, in the middle, manically attempting to cut them up as they roll past. The kids will love this bit – just keep them at a safe distance. You may also want to wear some kind of protective gloves too.

After a frantic 5 minutes chopping at whatever moves collect the decimated remains of your vegetables or meat and hurl them, whilst skating around the slippery kitchen, into a large pot of boiling fat. The pot should preferably be left teetering on the side of the cooker to simulate the constant terror of being horribly burnt as the 'kitchen boat' lurches around uncontrollably. Throw in a sauce of your choice. Encourage the kids to keep rolling random food up and down the floor or work surfaces while you try to stir the odd concoction without getting 1st degree burns. Remember they can improvise with tins from the cupboard too.

Next, get a second pot going, this time overfilled to the brink with hot water, which hopefully will slosh over realistically when it gets to boiling point. Again, throw the pasta / rice / potatoes from a distance into this second pot whilst hurtling around your kitchen. Try to dodge the tins and sacks of flour the kids have now managed to get out and are happily rolling up and down. I told you they'd love it. Keep skating around for 30 minutes, you can take a break occasionally from the chaos by clinging to the oven hood cover just above the dangerously teetering boiling pots. This keeps up the constant fear of injury whilst giving you a breather from dodging the kids' latest discovery, the jars of jam and peanut butter.

After 30 minutes of this, you are now allowed to attempt to drain the pasta/potatoes/rice and in desperation pour the contents of the first pot into that of the second. Don't be alarmed, the end is in sight. Politely ask your kids to stop rolling stuff around and sit nicely at the table since the 'marine meal' is almost ready. Tell them to get their own bowls because you're feeling tired and stressed. Alert your husband/wife/friend at the end of the line to get ready to simulate an unpredictable rogue wave. Skate towards the serving table frantically clutching your enormous pot of superheated stew. Just before you get to the table shout "Now!" The line-handler will suddenly pull you away from the table, the physical laws of motion will kick in, the pot will leave your hands as you hurtle backwards, your kids will scream and dinner will be strewn all over your newly cleaned floor. Next, mop up the food and serve with a flourish. Believe you me, the look you give your kids at this stage will ensure they eat it all up without a single grumble. Finally, collapse in a heap. Congratulations. You have now completed your first lesson in cooking on board a boat without ever having left dry land.

After a couple more days of taking watches and enjoying creating 'marine meals', John decided he really wasn't happy at all and threatened he was going to 'friggin swim for it' by which I assumed 'it' being the land some miles away. The long term forecast deteriorated as we sailed past Crete, so we diverted to the historic ancient city of Chania to release Joiner John back to the world. He declared that he now had, in his opinion, already reached the stage of exalted Master Mariner and had earned enough sailing stories and anecdotes for a lifetime. Looking at the forecast we agreed he'd earned his stripes and the last we saw of John was of him disappearing into the nearest Cretan pub to take up his new post by the bar to provide entirely unasked for advice and assistance to all yachties within hailing distance.

Beating up the Rhodes Channel I was surprised and impressed with a passing local fishing boat that actually hailed us on the VHF to warn us the weather wasn't looking good. I thanked him for his concern and assured him we had updated weather information and would have another look at the options. A rare event of grotty yachties and fishermen being nice to each other. Reduced to three and without the assistance of Joiner John we nevertheless decided to push on keen to get to our final destination, Fethiye in Turkey. As the wind escalated swiftly to a good Force 8 (which means it was blowing a hoolie) I couldn't help but contemplate that John would have much preferred being out here, square-jawed and steadfast, than safe and sound nursing a beer or two in a warm and cosy Cretan bar berating anyone in a sailing jacket for their lack of steely nautical resolve.

But such, I suppose, is the burden of experience.

GONE FISHIN'

It is New Year's Eve. La Rochelle. Deep in France's stormy Bay of Biscay.

Jimmy and I are sitting in the saloon of a shiny brand new 40ft catamaran valued at around a million dollars. The vessel is securely tied up in probably the biggest marina in the world, La Port des Minimes, which comfortably holds thousands of yachts of all shapes and sizes. As we sit and stare gloomily at each other, outside the rain is hammering down on the decks and windows of the boat with a breath-taking ferocity. The storm outside is so strong we are being blown around on our berth like a cork in a barrel despite the multiple lines holding us alongside the pontoon. It has been raining like this since we turned up.

Since the vessel is tied up on the 'visitor berthing area' we are also near the entrance, so are subject to the regular sweep of the tide pouring in and then, 6 hours or so later, rushing out again further increasing our sense of movement. The vessel is constantly creaking and straining at her lines madly attempting to free herself to smash to pieces on the huge harbour walls protecting us from the worst of the raging elements.

Inside, with one small but valiant electric heater trying and failing to fight back against the French winter we sit glumly in a semi-circle staring mutely at each other: alongside us there's Ivan our 3rd crew member from Estonia by way of Russia, with proud Cossack blood flowing through his veins, Ivan is perhaps more immune to the cold than most but even he never appears without multiple layers and his ubiquitous woollen cap. Next to him, Jimmy is wearing a T-shirt. You can just make out the words 'Barnstonworth United' on it, the rest of the legend has long since worn away. Next to Jimmy on the curved internal settee, sits Harry the owner who appears remarkably content to sit in frozen silence staring bleakly out at the hammering storm. An enthusiastic and lively 70 year old, Harry has not been put off by the weather outside nor the cold inside, because his heart is warmed by the knowledge that, by eating and drinking on board this New Year's evening, he is saving a considerable sum of money. For contractual reasons too obscure to decipher even by the most talented Harvard litigators, we have agreed I am responsible for buying all the food on board. And Harry likes to eat well. A man of considerable wealth, Harry has long ago forgotten just how many American East Coast houses he now owes ("is it six or seven? Gawd, I can't remember myself to be honest") but by being an expert in contract law, even unpaid crew like Jimmy and poverty-stricken new recruit Ivan, have rumbled around in their meagre salt lined pockets for some spare shekels to buy this evening's wine. It is New Year's Eve after all, a time of giving and, for Harry at least, receiving.

We sit in mute contemplation. As the condensation silently freezes inside the windowpanes of the saloon, I am dimly aware we have been sitting and staring at each other for countless days now without seemingly moving or speaking. Occasionally our eyes rotate to our hopelessly brave little heater spluttering its heart out fighting off the impending Gallic freeze and for a time it does seem to make headway in the saloon itself, as, motionless, we find ourselves as the day progresses beginning to thaw, only to then feel compelled to descend at the end of each evening into the bowels of the twin hulled floating fridge to lie prone like frozen fish fingers in our bunks. Each night, as I lie on my bunk shivering through my teeth and watching my breath crystallise before me, I remind myself once again. It didn't have to be this way.

Before flying out to France I had checked the long-term forecast and could see only death and destruction squeezed between the numerous tightly packed isobars hurling themselves into Biscay on the forecasting website I tend to use. I had discussed delaying our departure until the weather improved. There was no rhyme or reason to fly in, I argued, we'd just be stuck in La Rochelle for weeks (lovely place though it no doubt is). No, you must come I was told. So, I went. Having met our new and super keen Russian/Estonia crew member at Southampton, the diminutive but very fit Ivan, Jimmy and I arrived in the cute little airport outside La Rochelle and were promptly met by the owner, Harry himself. Upon questioning Harry had immediately confirmed that the French team responsible for fitting out and finishing off the brand new vessel were now on holiday and, no, the boat wasn't finished yet and, no, they weren't coming back until after the New Year and no there was no chance of leaving until all their work had been completed anyway. Then he turned towards me enthusiastically

"When are you going provisioning? Because I could really do with some decent food on board, ya know – I've already been stuck in this gawd-damned Frenchie town for weeks".

I responded as respectfully as I could that, traditionally at least, the vessel owner covers the onboard costs (and, it has to said, the 'going out' costs too) for his skipper and crew. It was, I pointed out, 'A great and venerable Tradition of the Sea' that yacht owners are proud to support by 'looking after' the dietary requirements of their hard working and devoted crew. Harry looked aghast:

"Gawd, I only got you guys in because you covered the food, otherwise I would have gotten those Dutch fellas instead".

Jimmy's eyes widened a touch and he frowned to himself. For Jimmy this was a display of strong and passionate emotion. Harry waved his contract excitedly at me and I had to confess, upon perusal, it did indeed look like they'd been some kind of a bizarre deal made.

    I called the office. Yes, they confirmed, there had been a confusion over the small print of the multiple agreed contracts and no, there was now unfortunately no way around it without lengthy courtroom dramas, expensive legal fees and no doubt people in strange white wigs shouting at each other in Latin. I would have to pay. And that included tonight's wine too apparently.

In hindsight the mix up with the food budget didn't come as a particular surprise. Right from the first it was clear from our tentative pre-delivery email exchanges that Harry wasn't your 'average yacht owner' although I'm aware that's a pretty nebulous catch-all in itself. You see the unusual thing about Harry that slowly crept up on all of us as the journey progressed was that he didn't appear to be particularly interested in the sailing bit about owning a sailing boat. As time wore on, he showed little to no curiosity in our route, the planning, technical or navigational details of getting a small boat all the way from France to Grenada in the Caribbean or indeed any other aspect of the voyage. Setting sails and steering a course were all a mystery, as was manoeuvring the vessel under power. The rules of the road, the complex set of instructions to avoid smashing into another boat or just using the VHF radio weren't of any real consequence. Nothing wrong with any of that of course, I mean, that's why we were on board wasn't it? It just struck us as odd, when initially stepping inside the vessel there wasn't a single indication, no tell-tale books, almanacs, 'pilot' books, tourist information, island courtesy flags, charts or any other sign that this boat was about to embark on a 4500 mile voyage from France all the way to the 'Islands' as Harry mysteriously referred to the Caribbean. Perhaps he had some other 'islands' in mind. Like the 'islands' just offshore La Rochelle for instance. Upon reflection perhaps those WERE the islands he had in mind. No wonder he was generally so puzzled by our lack of apparent progress to the final destination.

No, it slowly became apparent to Jimmy, Ivan and I that Harry had bought this brand-new sailing vessel for one reason and one reason only. Not to sail but to go fishing. Because Harry liked to fish. Harry liked to fish a lot. Which is fine of course, no law against it, it was just more normal to buy a little fishing boat and potter around fishing in it, that's all. So, we did go fishing. Not around the waters outside La Rochelle or sneaking into little bays dotted around the nearby and very beautiful Ile de Re. No, we went fishing – across the Atlantic Ocean.

But first we had to sort out what Harry had and hadn't bought in preparation. The first couple of days on board, despite the wind howling round our ears, were actually quite productive.

As per every trip we had a long and comprehensive list of things nautical to check and tick off. One thing on our detailed list were 'Sails' and we soon found that, in addition to the more tradition fore and aft ones already rigged on the mast, we had a very large and expensive 'cruising chute'.

Now cruising chutes come in all shapes and sizes and also, helpfully, appear to have multiple nautical names. This helps confuse non-nautical types and makes the owner sound really professional and a 'serious sailor' to boot. So instead of one name you have 'Top Down Furler', 'Gennaker', 'Asymmetric Spinnaker', 'Cruising Chute', 'Kite' and even abbreviations too like 'MPS' (that's Multi-Purpose Sail). I personally find it helps to occasionally throw in references to 'Code Zeros' too just to mix it up a bit. Even better, proper job racers will use baffling sub-terms for which 'Chute' to employ like A5, A3 or A1 and will also give the huge things pseudonyms like 'Big Boy' or 'Grandma's Knickers' to help confuse the issue further. And Harry had got confused, and I for one couldn't blame him. Upon closer inspection we discovered this lightweight and voluminous canvas was a 'Top Down Furler' which was just great, but it quickly emerged there was a problem.

These large cruising sails come with a drum with a continuous line on them, the drum spins like crazy when you release the furling line to get the sail spinning out and, when you want to furl the huge bloody thing back in, just haul away on the line and it will furl itself away by spinning back around itself. No problem. But we didn't have a top down furler drum, we had a standard little French one that was designed for a standard little French cruising chute not the enormous racing gennaker that Harry had flown in, at great expense, to assist him in getting to 'the Islands'. The salesman had done a great job shifting thousands of dollars of sail. It just wouldn't work that's all and would only lead to much screaming, shouting, bashing and general gnashing of teeth as is the Great Tradition of the Sea.

Anyway, with time to kill before the French yard returned from their 'vacances', we thought we'd give it a shot so, in a brief respite from the howling wind, when all suddenly became very still and quiet, we attached this sizeable monster to a line and our sturdy little furler drum and hauled it up the mast. Then all hell broke loose. Even in a flat calm and with the considerable help of Jimmy's remarkable strength, we struggled to get the demented enormous monster to furl back around itself on the little furler drum we had been supplied. It just wasn't right. A new super-duper top down furling drum plus the other rather important missing component, a flexible but sturdy bit of rig that the sail wraps itself around know as a 'torque line', would have to be sent all the way from America.

"We can just FedEx it – it will be here in 24 hours no problem", Harry confidently predicted. I tried to suggest making use of the firm's local guys here in La Rochelle, one of the biggest sailing centres in Europe, but to no avail. The new kit would be sent from the States. And it would take over a week. And then be impounded by the central post office in Lisbon.

After 10 days staring at the rain and feeding Harry's considerable need for expensive food and wine it suddenly cleared up, the French boat yard sprang magically to life, and before we knew it, we were on our way. By the time, that is around 60 seconds, it took us to pass through the marina entrance into the main channel out of La Rochelle Harry was enthusiastically rigging multiple fishing rods from every conceivable corner of the boat. We were going to have fish for lunch, supper and breakfast. We were going to do our bit to deplete international fishing stocks around the world. The poor old shiny slippery little beauties of the deep wouldn't know what hit them. And sure enough, 24 hours later, we made our first catch. A huge ruddy great fishing net round our port side propeller and we limped into Gijon in northern Spain.

Manoeuvring a catamaran with only one engine may sound pretty easy right? I mean you still have one working engine don't you and, as long as you only need to turn one way, it's all good. No problem. Now if you want to turn the other way i.e. to the right when the working engine is on the right side, well, that's not so easy. In fact, it ain't going happen. Throw in night-time, a dazzling array of background lights and a new, unfamiliar marina plunged into darkness and that's when the fun really starts. In the event we got in fine. Even Jimmy looked relieved.

Gijon (pronounced hee-hon like in Donkey speak) is one of those superb northern Spanish cities that is almost entirely unknown outside Asturias, let alone Spain. After safely securing the vessel and agreeing that, in the dark and all tired out, now was not the time to look into our 'prop wrap' we ventured into the old town area of Gijon which is right on the doorstep of the handy marina we'd tentatively manoeuvred ourselves into that evening. As we began exploring the bars and restaurants of the narrow isthmus that divides the old town, we emerged into a huge bay overlooked by an ancient Roman Catholic church. The surf came crashing into this Bay and it soon became apparent that Gijon was basically one huge surfer's paradise. During the day there was a multitude of them all kitted out in wet suits and happily surfing away, riding waves seemingly right into the centre of town. It was like some ancient surfer community had decided to create the perfect curved beach with guaranteed breakers supplied courtesy of the Bay of Biscay and then build a beautiful and striking Spanish city around the surfers play area as a visually pleasing historical backdrop.

The other striking discovery we made that evening was that Gijon appeared to be the cheap cider capital of the world. Wandering aimlessly into a bar called La Galana on the Plaza Major we were immediately struck by the huge barrels of cider mounted around the large room and at the same time our sense of smell was assaulted by the strong slightly acidic smell of multiple fermented apples. Swiftly observing that this was 'his kind of place' Jimmy immediately ordered a bottle of the local green cider, and, on establishing the remarkable cost involved, promptly and generously ordered us all a bottle each.

Apparently, they were pretty much giving the stuff away. Harry Heaven.

There was a snag though – our waiter insisted that we weren't allowed to pour our own drinks, it had to be done properly, by holding the bottle above your head, looking straight ahead with as blank an expression as possible and then tip it slowly and deliberately into your glass held around waist height. Although we all admired the blank expression, and the skill and agility involved, it did mean a large amount of the precious fluid ended up on the floor – hence explaining the strong stench when we first entered. The floor, tables and the bar itself was soaked in the stuff. The rest of the evening passed in a cider strewn haze and, for a while at least, we all forgot about prop wraps and lousy weather and top down furlers too – that is, until we woke the next morning with the sour smell of fermented apples in our clothes and remembered we had a problem to resolve.

The waters of the Bay of Biscay can of course be very pleasant to swim in in summer. No doubt holidaying on the coast in July or August may well include frolicking around with a refreshing but fun splash in the sun-drenched blue stuff. However, this wasn't bucolic summer but frozen winter, the start of a New Year and no one, beside the heavily wet suited surfers on the other side of town, goes into the water. At first we valiantly attempted to remove the mass tangled cordage with chopping knives manfully strapped to our boat hook, but it soon became obvious someone would need to take the plunge, go into the water itself, to cut the huge, confused line off our propeller. Harry enthusiastically suggested Ivan, since, steeped in the great traditions of enduring Russian winters, a dive in the murky freezing waters of northern Spain in winter would be a 'stroll in the Red Square' in comparison for our redoubtable Cossack crew member. For his part Ivan looked less convinced.

I got the marina to book a diver who promptly turned up sporting thick full body wet suit and mask. He looked a tough and hardy local who knew exactly what he was about. Which was when Harry intervened:

"How much is this guy goin' charge for this anyhow?"

Having discovered the price, a reasonable amount I thought, Harry declared he would be damned if he paid that much and would buy his own wet suit and dive in himself and still have some money left over for a barrel of cider. Jimmy and I demurred, quietly looking forward to being observers of this heroic act, and Harry went off to buy his wet suit.

He was soon back, with just the top, no doubt saving considerable money by buying half a wet suit. We all looked on blankly as Harry made preparations for just freezing his lower body, I guess he considered that half expendable, an unnecessary appendage that could be sacrificed for the good of the voyage. Looking on, and suspecting an important lesson was about to be learnt, I began to warm to the idea myself and made nice hot cups of tea for the spectators so we could adopt a pleasant pose to observe the dive from the safety of our al fresco dining area. Harry, half dressed for the occasion, began his preparations by dipping his left toe into the water. The look of dawning horror is one I'll cherish for a while. Which is when Ivan, looking on compassionately, ruined it all by volunteering to sacrifice himself instead. A new recruit to this game and keen to impress, Ivan had been stirred to heroism – like I said, new to this game.

"Well that's a damn fine idea Ivan! Heck, dinner's on me if you get that line free" beamed a clearly relieved Harry.

Jimmy sighed and began rubbing the top of his nose in quiet rumination whilst little Ivan gingerly donned the half a wet suit and slipped into the freezing waters.

I must confess I was not happy with how things were developing. Call me an old-fashioned hack but I do prefer to keep crew alive on trips if only to make me look good – and this wasn't looking good. Ivan, hell bent on impressing us all soon began to turn an interesting shade of blue as he insisted on diving again and again into the arctic waters, half-clad whilst hacking away at the impressive fishing line surrounding the propeller. He was clearly making headway however, with little pieces of torn line drifting off across the marina but we watched with mounting concern at the colour of his increasingly blue legs kicking back under the boat for 'just one more dive' to Harry's cries of ecstatic encouragement.

For his part Jimmy was becoming increasingly animated. Striding up and down huffing and puffing with discontent he didn't need to say a word. It was clear this was dangerously wrong, and I told Ivan in no uncertain words to get his rear end back on board immediately:

"Just one more go skipper" was Ivan's gasping reply as he plunged back under the stern of the vessel with Harry excitedly encouraging him to ever more valiant acts. I was on the verge of grabbing our foolishly heroic Russian by the heels and dragging him back on board myself when he finally emerged, final piece of line in hand, triumphant and quiet clearly showing the early signs of hypothermia. Jimmy and I dragged him shivering out of the water whilst Harry ran off to force alcohol down his throat – which is probably the worst possible thing you can do for someone with all the signs of cold water hypothermia and we got the little chap into the relative warmth of the cabin with a warm shower running.

That evening Harry, as promised, took us in triumph to the most expensive restaurant he could find and, taken aback by this surprising turn of events, we enthusiastically ordered steaks all round whilst privately thinking that we had perhaps unjustly misread our wealthy American boat owner. With Harry enthusiastically ordering wine bottle after wine bottle the evening was marked by much good-natured banter and general bonhomie. Until the Bill turned up that is:
"Hell, I ain't paying for you guys! Just Ivan here".
Ahh.

We left the next day and made our way slowly west and then, passing Finisterre, turned south to rendezvous with our Fedex gennaker furling kit and super-duper torque line in Cascais just outside Lisbon. Which hadn't turned up yet, and when it did, five long days later was immediately impounded by Portuguese customs for VAT reasons. Not that Cascais is an unpleasant place to be delayed of course. If you're ever stuck in Cascais waiting for ship's parts (which of course you'll never be) you can always jump on a bus to Sintra in the mountains to the north to explore one of the most crazy Moorish castles on the planet – perched ridiculously above the town its complex snake-like circuit of walls seems to defy gravity itself. Alternatively, you can pop into Lisboa itself and wander aimlessly around this very pleasantly compact and welcoming capital city – watch out for the trams though. They don't take any prisoners.

When our long-awaited parts were finally retrieved from customs Harry threw the large box onboard and declared we should leave immediately. I tentatively suggested it may be an idea to actually see what was in the box BEFORE we left for the Canary Islands and after much fiddling around we agreed that the contents did indeed look like what had been ordered without really establishing whether all the component parts; the enormous sail itself, the furling gear and the magical 'torque line' would all work together. I suggested we made use of the local representative of the huge international sailmaker to help ensure all was right before we left. No – no more time wasting was possible I was told. The delay had cost enough. That test would have to come later. When it was too late.

La Palma is one of the westernmost Canary Islands that people generally ignore in favour of the more famous Lanzarote, Tenerife and Gran Canaria. I suppose this is partially because the islands further west tend to get more rain than those holiday hotspots to the east, the result being the western islands are greener, cleaner and largely unspoilt whilst the eastern islands are hot, arid and generally pretty crowded. In short best keep away from those pesky western islands and stick with the hot spots – you wouldn't like them. Terrible places. Honest. Anyway we rolled up in the island's capital, Santa Cruz, in late evening about a week out from Cascais and found so many spare spaces in the marina to choose from I immediately plumped on the space most likely to be asked to be moved from. By the time the agitated marina assistant had tracked me, Jimmy and Ivan down to the bar overlooking the marina we were already on to our third beer and therefore were unable to comply with his frenzied requests to move the vessel being impaired from an insurance, legal and also practical point of view. Ivan just sat next to us cherishing his bottle and grinning inanely, occasionally chuckling to himself in Russian. Perhaps his over-lengthy exposure to the chilling waters of Biscay had had a permanent affect?

It had been a good run and, on our way down in very light and cautious breezes, we had tested out Harry's super expensive gennaker. It took three of us sweating and swearing to furl the damn thing back on to itself – it just wasn't right, and I made a silent promise to myself never to try the enormous brute of a thing again. Well, not on my watch at least.

Santa Cruz, the capital of La Palma is simply stunning. An ancient trading port with characterful stone streets and secret alleyways left steaming in the morning sun after the occasional downpour – yes, it rains there occasionally but the result is a verdant and dramatic island with superb Pacific like redoubts that hover over Santa Cruz like some Hawaii volcanoes transported to the Atlantic. It's a bloody revelation. We spent a couple of days there restocking the vessel for the long passage ahead and privately wondering if our multi-millionaire owner would ever offer to buy a round one evening. We all agreed that, so far at least, the great transatlantic fishing expedition had been rather disappointing fish-wise. Harry, with the true enthusiasm of the zealot had avidly cast multiple lines out all day and every day from sunrise to sunset and we still hadn't caught a fish apart from a kamikaze flying fish, who, no doubt taking pity on us, had actually thrown itself on the deck as some form of heroic sacrifice for the common good. Flying fish make good eating if you top and tail them, gut them and fry them in olive oil with herbs / garlic of your choice but I couldn't face doing the same with this, our one solitary offering from Poseidon. I threw him back in. Can't stand suicidal fish. They depress me.

The classic voyage east to west from the Canaries to the Caribbean has the sailing nickname 'The Milk Run' because, the theory goes, it's just one long gentle sail downwind with all on deck sipping gin and tonic's whilst the ever-faithful autopilot (all sailors love autopilots – if they don't they're just fibbing) steers a steady and serene course to Grenada, St Lucia or the British Virgin Islands etc etc. The days are spent in a dream like slumber as the weather slowly becomes warmer and more idyllic, the nights starry eyed and soporific – a constant trance of beauty and ocean-going tranquillity. This is the popular view of the run to the Caribbean. For us it never stopped blowing like nuts on a string. I don't think 'nuts on a string' is a common nautical phrase, in fact I'm sure I just made it up, but you get the idea. 'Milk Run' my funicular, we spent the entire trip heavily reefed down and trying to stop the boat tearing itself to pieces in the process.

The good news with all this heavy wind was that there was absolutely no chance in hell we were going to unleash the 'top down furler enormous beasty sail' which I'd already promised to myself never to use again. When the damn thing ripped itself to smithereens Harry would be on to his lawyers in seconds filing multiple indictments against his reckless skipper for destroying his beautiful kite – no, wasn't falling for that one. Well, not this time at least. In the event we made it across in around 18 days which was a fine run all things considered and then, a few days before we arrived in Grenada, a miracle happened. Harry actually caught a fish.

Journeys end. Le Phare Blue. Grenada. Crystal clear water. Palm trees. Cute little beach by the bar. Sun drenched pontoons with a mild north-easterly breeze blowing gently enough to create the slow movement of water lapping against the hulls of a host of gleamingly white and thoroughly cleaned mono hulls and catamarans secured safely within this picture postcard marina on the south coast of Grenada. The wind-swept rain and storms of La Rochelle are now a distant and seemingly impossible memory. The frozen dives and stormy crossing are a thing of the past, inconceivable even. Reclining alongside an idyllic clear pool of water, cool beers in hand and at peace we can see our former vessel from our prone position near the bar. Thoroughly cleaned and cleared of all traces of us she sits awaiting her next adventure. Harry has already enthusiastically started making plans for more fishing trips after the recent successful triumph. Given the task of clearing us in with immigration he has managed to immediately lose all our passports only for me to find them still sitting on a desk in the passport office a frantic hour later. Panic over, our bags are packed, off the boat and we've a moments calm before the taxi comes to whisk us away to the airport and return us to our lives back home.

Jimmy lies on a sunbed next to me as we recline by the swimming pool laid on for marina guests. Jimmy's enormous beer belly is out proudly on display to all, his funny skinny little legs poking out beneath like embarrassed toothpicks, a cold Carib in his hand, I notice his voluminous light blue swimming trunks have little anchors on them. Ivan is lying close by but in the shade, looking around him in wonder. Inexplicably he still has his little black woollen hat on. His body language suggests one message: 'So THIS is the Caribbean then?!'

Inevitably the bar is playing some reggae music but, since it is between lunch and dinner, the volume is discreet for once. This is a quiet place away from the madness of modernity and it's all ours just for a moment. Just a moment.

"So, he bought lunch then?" says Jimmy suddenly. I turn and look at him.

"Well, since we all deliberately wandered off and went swimming before the bill turned up, I guess he didn't have much choice, did he?" I smiled.

"A couple of sandwiches and some coke? What did it come to?"

"Around 20 dollars I guess".

Jimmy took a sip of his ice-cold beer and sighed.

"Tight bastard" he said.

Some people are never happy.

THIS SAILING LIFE

"How about fuel?" I asked.

"Oh, almost full I'd say". The owner, a sailing veteran, has lived on and sailed this boat for countless years. What he doesn't know about his boat isn't worth knowing.
"Almost full?"
"About 80%"
"And the fuel gauge, is it accurate?"
"Mmmm, tends to drop fast but it's good". I looked at the fuel gauge. It was showing full beyond the max limit and made a quick calculation. That would give us around 175 litres which would get us a fair distance whilst we had no wind. We could at least get going and make some progress north past the Algarve

and start punching our way up the Portuguese coast – always a bit of a struggle since the current and prevailing wind is invariably against you as you try to get up the coast but we could make a start at least. Jimmy, perched next to me, grunted approvingly.

We were sitting in a marina just off Cadiz, southwest Spain, and we were leaving soon for Plymouth, England. A port I've strangely never been to but had passed by countless times. An old and rather tired French built boat. Jimmy and I plus our new Polish crew, Christian, had already worked our way through the vessel; noting problems, photographing any issues, resolving what we could and then had the pleasure of fixing both loos that we had found leaking unspeakable things. Welcome to the exotic sailing life we lead.

Christian, a blue-eyed hard-working Pole with an open honest face and very pleasant almost childlike manner had joined us for the sail back to Blighty. With our preparations complete and reasonably content that the vessel was relatively seaworthy we left, after a night out locally to forge our common but always temporary brotherhood, heading out across the Bay of Cadiz towards the Cape of St Vincent, the southwesternmost point of Europe.

As I came up on deck that evening with the engine chuntering away happily, I found our earnest Pole deep into a monologue with Jimmy listening on attentively with his sympathetic look on. Christian appeared to be reliving some form of hellish sweatshop existence from his distant past:

"So, then the Boss...he says to me 'clean the shower!' So, I clean the shower. Is already very clean but when he say 'clean' I clean."

Christian opened his hands in a placatory manner.

"So, I clean all morning. The shower is very clean now. So, he come in, and say 'clean again', I say, 'but IS clean', he say, 'now clean with toothbrush'".

Christian looked up at us with his startlingly blue eyes and smiled apologetically holding his open palms up again and gives a little laugh.

"So, he give me toothbrush and I start to clean again, cleaning, you know, in the little grooves on the floor but now with little toothbrush".

Jimmy pulled a concerned face and made supportive soothing noises.

"Then he say, 'clean hull' so I dive in and clean hull".

"With a toothbrush?!" I ask.

"No, not toothbrush, with big brush."

Christian gives us his big childlike grin.

"Like deck brush. But I no swim too good, get very tired. I say, 'I can't swim too good, Boss, tired.' Boss say 'Idiot. Use diving equipment', so I use diving equipment".

"Can you dive Christian?" I asked.

"Ah no, never. Boss shows me how to put on mask, take tank and weight belts and dive in again. Say it no problem."

Christian grinned in his boyish manner and then continued with a little frown beginning to form on his innocent face.

"But I don't find it too easy. It not so easy to dive, not as easy as I thought. I keep going down, down, down and then I hit bottom" He paused.

"You sunk to the bottom?!"

"Yes, but got back up again… well, not so easy."

Out Polish friend paused suddenly and looked over the sea with a faraway distant frown. He shook himself.

"Then I clean hull".

Christian looked up at us again with his innocent smile then he waggled his head. "So, I clean all day, every day over and over again on boat that is already sparkling clean and sometimes Boss hit me on head".

"He hit you on your head?!"

"Yes, with deck brush. Always hitting head and saying, 'Now you clean this' and 'Now you clean that'. It was strange but good money", he made his big innocent grin and opened up his hands again.

"When on Earth was this Christian?" I asked incredulously.

"Oh, last week. On super yacht. I was deck crew for 6 months in Antibes."

Super yacht crews are a rare breed of masochists even by sailing industry standards. They all tend to be well qualified sailors with RYA 'Ocean Yachtmasters' and 'MCA class 4 tickets' and 'STCW' thingies springing out of their ears that all sound very impressive and professional. Strolling along the lines of super yachts, mega yachts and giga yachts in places like Palma, Majorca or Antibes on the Cote d'Azur you'll see these crews parading around with cool shades on, spotless whites and perhaps a cool walkie talkie on their belt. But instead of envying their glamorous lives take a moment to pity the poor lost souls. Since, despite their impressive lists of qualifications, all they do all day, and are allowed to do all day, as far as I can see at least, is function as modern day slaves. Well, servants perhaps since they actually get paid and that.

I had a friend once who'd done his time in the Army who landed the 'dream job' on a super yacht which pressed all the most desirable buttons – good pay, an action packed itinerary travelling to the world's most exotic locations, the owner a lovely old man, the captain a great guy and the boat itself was one of the most beautiful sailing yachts on the planet. And, after 4 months on board, he couldn't stand it anymore and quit. Why? Because, according to him, the Army has nothing, absolutely nothing on super yacht work for reducing you to feeling like the lowest possible micro-organism on the planet. Be in no doubt, you may have nice sunglasses and sport a great tan after hanging around in Antigua for a while, but the honest reality is you are in the great scheme of things beneath an amoeba and for God's sake don't think of talking to the owner and his guests, in fact don't even look at them or you'll have your eyes put out with a red hot poker.

On top of this it's also probably the most sexist and ageist organisation left in the world. There are countless super yachts in the world run by countless men in white shorts crewed by pretty blondes of a certain age and shape. Female skippers are almost unheard of and heaven forbid you grow older than, say, 30 – out you go to pasture, or the knacker's yard, you poor old thing you.

Anyway, there we were motoring along in the gulf of Cadiz feeling like we were some kind of rescue service for ex-super yacht crew. That evening after we had fed and watered Christian and put him to bed to recuperate with Jimmy sitting by his bunk patting him reassuringly on his calloused hands, I took the midnight to 3am watch, the graveyard shift, and took the opportunity to observe our fuel gauge. It was resolutely still showing 'full' with no apparent shift in any direction at all despite us motoring all day. Now anyone out there that is familiar with yachts will tell you that most things onboard will fail sooner or later at some time or other on a yacht at sea. The water and fuel tank gauges aren't like this. They fail sooner and all the time every day. In short, I didn't trust the damn thing and, despite the advice of our helpful owner, immediately changed direction to the nearest fuel dock, in this case, Portimao on the Algarve coast.

Overnight we continued to motor through a flat calm sea. We arrived that morning and chugged straight up to the refuelling station. Now I knew from the makers specification of this vessel that we had a total capacity of 200 litres. We began filling her up and when the tank was almost ready to overflow I checked how much we'd put in on the pump's gauge – it read 196 litres. The fuel gauge didn't budge of course and, having opened up the tank to inspect the gauge itself, discovered that that was because it didn't actually have one. It had long since corroded away. Christian for his part seemed surprised by this discovery; Jimmy and I were more sanguine perhaps. In fact after years of doing this job I'm pleasantly surprised if the owners know anything at all about their pride and joy – I'm constantly amazed at their blissful ignorance in fact, but again, I guess that's why we're there, so not complaining, just intrigued that's all.

I did a job once where the owner, a lovely fellow, swore blind that there was only one filter on his diesel engine because he'd had the whole thing religiously serviced by pros for years now. In all their years on board he'd assured me they'd never found or serviced the primary filter since there obviously wasn't one, instead focussing on the fine fuel filter on the engine itself and none other. Puzzled by this but reassured by his insistence we got going. And sure enough the engine died. Because the primary filter was so gunked up by seven years or so of collecting all the filth from the fuel tank, that it refused to allow any more fuel through before it was changed. The poor thing, sitting happily beneath the owner's bed, literally beneath his feet, had finally given up the ghost after many, many years of dutiful service.

The fact that the damn thing decided to die on me in 20 knots of breeze, 10 metres from a safe harbour within a wind trap that was nigh on impossible to sail out of in the world's most un-sailable vessel left me with the only option of attempting to 'drop the hook' there and then. Unfortunately, we found the anchor that we had tested in port only a couple of days before had now decided to seize up when we really needed it which left us with the only option of sailing out of trouble on a boat that simply refused to sail to windward. The closely anchored vessels one side, the great ruddy harbour walls on the other and a beckoning lee shore behind helped focus the mind too. Well, we made it, of course, in about a thousand 'tacks', which means taking the nose through the wind including 'wearing' the boat multiple times, which means taking the arse through the wind when the nose can't be arsed or something like that. Anyway it was the nearest damn thing. Boy, did we enjoy our vanilla rums that evening. But, well, you get the gist anyway. Owners don't necessarily know their boats very well. Sometimes not at all. But that's this sailing life all over. And there's more puzzling aspects to the strange world of mucking about on boats too. Take, for instance, that rare breed of sailor, the Round the World Racers.

Round the World Solo Sailors. The titanic heroes of my sport, the demi-gods of the ocean deservedly feted and praised wherever they go. And they deserve it too. What they do isn't easy, not easy at all. And it takes guts and stamina and technical expertise and a certain obsessive hell-for-leather bloody-mindedness that most of us retiring mortals lost, or more likely, never possessed in the first place. Their endeavours are rewarded with knighthoods, damehoods and fame and perhaps even a little fortune (although not much let's be honest).

The first chap to sail alone around the world was an American called Joshua Slocum, back in 1895. He wrote a terrific book about it, in which he fought off natives with carpet tacks, ate dodgy plums off the Azores and ended up hallucinating that his boat was being steered by one of

Christopher Columbus's own navigators in ghostly form. All great stuff and from a literary point of view at least quite inspirational. Anyway he proved once and for all it was possible to sail solo round the world and only go a bit crazy in the process. In 1909 he set sail again, off up the Amazon and, not surprisingly, was never heard of again. I'd like to think he met a nice local girl, settled down, gave up messing around on the water and raised a family but suspect that wasn't what actually happened unfortunately.

Turn the clock forward to 1966 and another chap called Francis Chichester also sailed around the world alone, kept off the plums and got back in one piece which was great until someone pointed out he'd been mad enough to actually stop for a bit, in Australia, which meant the whole thing was a disaster – although they knighted him anyway. Which was nice. A couple of years later another Brit called Robin Knox Johnson proved you could sail around the world non-stop with or without plums and without actually stopping at all (perish the thought) by sailing from Falmouth in the UK to Falmouth in the UK via everywhere else. He was also knighted which was also very nice. At the end of the race he gave his entire winnings (it was a Sunday Times funded race) to the poor wife of a chap who did actually go mad on the same race, a gesture which, in my book, was actually a more impressive thing to do than 'sailing around the world non-stop' so I would have knighted him for being a ruddy fine generous chap but then again I'm not the Queen. But here we come to the whole problem of the thing and that is sailing around the world without stopping is a very odd thing to do.

If, for instance, I proposed to my mates down the pub one evening that I intended to fly around the world without stopping they would quite rightly ask:

"Why would anyone do that? That's nuts".

They may go on to observe that such a futile task was relatively easy and also entirely pointless – I mean, what's the point of going around this huge and fascinating globe with all its varied places and peoples without actually stopping and meeting the locals or exploring the nearest castle/temple/interesting rock or whatever, popping into a nice restaurant and tasting the local cuisine or having a beer and watching the sun go down? It strikes me as perhaps the most pointless thing to do. So, I say:

"Then why sail around the world without stopping? Surely that's just as nuts?"

"Aahhh, but it's the challenge, the physical constraints and danger", my sailing friends say, which is, of course, true. So, I propose to not only fly from London to London but give myself a dangerous physical challenge along the way by repeatedly beating my head against the coach roof of the plane every, shall we say, 30 mins en route.

"Surely", I point out, "I should be knighted upon my return, if I did in fact manage to return, after such a hazardous enterprise?"

We all ruminate on this for a bit. After a discussion, we all agree that flying round the world non-stop repeatedly hitting your head would not be an easy thing to do and could quite possibly lead to heavy concussion, brain damage and some very odd looks indeed from my fellow passengers to boot. But another friend wouldn't have it.

"It's about the SPEED you go you see" he points out. "I mean if you manage to sail across the entire Atlantic in just 5 days then you'd be a hero, a titan and be rightly fêted etc, etc."

To which I responded that I for one HAVE crossed the Atlantic quicker than that, in 8 hours actually, on a plane. I contend that if the purpose is to get across the Atlantic Ocean as quickly as possible, why on earth would you go by a silly little sailing boat?

I mean, what's the point in that? Jump on the plane for Christ's sake! But my words fall on deaf ears.

Still I'd like to be the first sailor to cross the Atlantic on a boat made entirely of fudge. I mean, imagine that? I'd be a fudge-loving bloody hero...

The wind got up and we started sailing. Sailing boats are designed to sail, not motor, and our speed started picking up nicely. It's also a wonderful release from the constant drone of the engine. I've known crew driven mad by the constant whine of the engine. I had one once which emitted a strange high pitched and maddingly alternating buzzing sound (engine that is, not crew). We were mid-Atlantic and had to motor for a long time in a flat calm. It almost drove me absolutely crackers. I ended up sitting on the bow to get as far away from it as was safely possible and stop the boat turning into an aquatic version of The Shining. Luckily, the wind returned before anyone started attacking cabin doors with axes shouting, 'Skipper's home'.

All things good (and bad) must come to an end though so, after a pleasant sail north overnight the following morning the wind died halfway up the coast to Lisbon, so we tried to start the engine again. Of course, it wouldn't go. Now I'm not going to bore you senseless with why it wouldn't start, it was something to do with the fuel supply but God knows what and anyway it was rather dull then, even more dull to recount now. Bloody engines, almost took the axe to it, but realised that might alarm Christian - poor chap had suffered enough I thought.

So, we drifted around a bit and tried to work the problem. We tried lots of things. Jimmy is particularly good with engines. You'll have to trust me on this. Everything we tried failed to start the engine. It left me quietly ruminating upon the amount of time Jimmy and I have spent just, well, drifting around. It's actually quite good for the soul drifting aimlessly around totally out of control for a while, literally going with the flow. It's not something people do lots of nowadays but perhaps we all should occasionally? Until the flow takes you towards a hard-rocky place, then it's less pleasant.

I once found myself drifting through the Raz De Sein on the Brittany coast in a dead calm and thick soupy fog. The Raz De Sein is not a place to enjoy drifting around contemplating your navel since it is covered in nasty sharp rocks and one of the most powerful tides on the planet. Guess it's fair to say I didn't have much time for quiet reflection then since Jimmy and I were busy performing the world's fastest fan belt change. We had already managed to put the fire out though, so things were looking up. They don't tell you about THAT at Boat Shows.

Anyway, eventually the wind picked up again, so we began sailing. My plan was to sail up to Cascais, off Lisbon, call up the marina when we were close, and they'd send a nice chap in a rib to tow us in. I prayed that the wind wouldn't die at the last moment. It didn't and we were towed in in triumph.

One of the golden rules of sailing is that, when you break down and are desperately in need of a mechanic or engineer, and whatever country you struggle into and whatever time of year you choose, there will always be a National Holiday on the day you arrive. If you're in a real rush the National Holiday will extend up to and over the weekend too. It is one of the Great Traditions of the Sea. It was a National Holiday that day too, of course, so we gave up trying to get help and went for a beer instead. Christian and Jimmy agreed that National Holidays were good things and I, for one, wasn't going to argue with them. When we could finally get a second opinion on the engine it emerged we had a faulty fuel supply/starter battery/alternator/leaky gasket cover issue on our hands. We fixed what we could and continued only to break down again off Porto and then break down again off Bayona. We broke down a lot on that trip and sometimes the engine failed too. More ominously the weather was closing in. Time was running out and autumn was swiftly turning into winter. Ahead the Bay of Biscay beckoned in its own uniquely welcoming way.

If you're going to break down Bayona is a good place to do just that. South of the city of Vigo in northwest Spain, Bayona sits on the east end of a large natural bay (or Ria as the locals would say) and presents a magnificent welcome to sailors cast ashore in despair. As you find yourself limping in, you'll pass a picture perfect Moorish Castle housing a large grand state run hotel Parador. Looking up to your right, you'll spot a remarkable Spanish Civil War era statue of a heroic Spanish maid, so big she holds a stone ship in her hands, beckoning you to safety, whilst ahead the town itself, with its classic large square windowed houses, overlooks some super cute little beaches which line the Bay. Those of a cultural bent can visit a fine replica of Columbus's ship, the Pinta, and, having sated your cultural instincts, can be lured happily into the secret hidden away backstreet bars and restaurants just behind the front. A delightful maze of little alleyways teeming with life after 8pm with a particularly good Mojito bar if you're ever passing. For those struggling in from the sea, the best plan is to tie up in the quite superb Monte Real Club de Yates and immediately decant to the large, classy leather sofa-lined cool interior of the club. If it's later in the day take a pew outside, order a gin and tonic and just take in the view of the sun setting over the Spanish Rias. Try to pretend you fit in.

Ahead of us lay the 'Costa del Muerte', the Coast of Death and the world-famous headland, Finisterre, literally, the End of the World. The Spaniards have a great knack with naming. No 'Cape of Good Hope' for them, it's all doom and gloom and inevitable destruction. But, relaxing as we were on the patio of the Monte Real Club de Yates with a gin and tonic in our hands, things weren't looking good. I think it's fair to say the faith we had had in the boat at the start had been reduced somewhat over the previous week or so. Perhaps it was something to do with the fact it kept breaking down and stank of human faeces? It is a general and very good rule for skippers never to be critical about 'the boat', if there's a problem it's up to you to fix it, not whine about it, and besides, it may hear you complaining about it and decide to sink just to prove the point.

Not that we're a superstitious lot of course. No, not at all. We got as much on the engine done as we could to get us going again and cracked on north. The forecast wasn't looking good though. It wasn't looking good at all.

A long ocean voyage is much like climbing a huge mountain. You don't do it one jump but tend to break in down into legs. In climbing there's establishing base camp, then camp one, camp two and so on ending, hopefully with the big push to the summit (and preferably back again). I tend to look at long coastal trips as a collection of headlands. You tick them off as you go, one headland at a time now, don't get too carried away. One by one, nice and steady. And always remember the golden rule, a good general knows when to retreat. This particular voyage's first milestone was safely rounding cape St Vincent, now far behind us, then past the surprisingly nasty double act of Raso and Roca off Lisbon. Now we sailed past Finisterre, then Torinana and really not very sweet looking Villano. We struggled valiantly past Sisargas, decided not to pull into La Coruna but keep cracking on. As we fought our way northeast the forecast kept looking worse and worse. Depression after depression was lining up to sweep across Biscay and the western approaches to the UK. Plymouth, our final destination, was still

450 nautical miles or so northwards but we'd run out of luck, not that we'd started with much. It wasn't going to happen this side of Christmas. When we stopped, we'd be stopped for good. Well weeks anyway. We tracked east along the northern Spanish coast looking for a safe harbour.

I've never heard of Ribadeo. You probably haven't too. Just outside the entrance is a cute little light house on the island of Pancha which you can stroll along to if you've just driven up in your car. Or smashed your boat on the rocks beneath. The short-lived winter sun was on its way down as we nervously looked astern to the gathering clouds to the west which gave us a pretty clear idea of what was on its way. Sometimes you don't need to be a meteorologist to know that the shit is about to hit the nautical fan, all you need to do is look at the clouds, see great big ruddy black ones come stampeding towards you, feel the wind on your face and sagely nod you head and sigh and say something entirely unnecessary like 'Oohh it'll blow like granny's knackers this evening'. On this occasion Jimmy opted for: "You wouldn't get much change out of THAT one" and we all knew exactly what he meant, although God knows where he got that one from too.

I decided on this occasion to avoid having too close a look at the lighthouse, sweet though it was, checked our mast wouldn't 'say hello' to the bridge crossing the entrance to the ria and, having digested the almanac's advice that 'tides run hard' around here and the not particularly reassuring 'depths may be less than charted' comment, we managed to manoeuvre ourselves on to a 'hammerhead' pontoon near the entrance, the 'hammerhead' being the big one at the end that is the easiest, in theory at least, to get yourself safely on to when 'the tides run hard' as real salty sailors would say. Being winter the marina wasn't exactly buzzing. In fact, it was quite a job to find anyone interested in us at all.

Arrival in a new marina having escaped the clutches of the sea always feels anticlimactic. You go from clinging on for dear life with the wind howling round your ears to dead boring calm in seconds and no one ashore gives a damn. Temperature wise, having put on all your spare clothes and dreading the quiet deadly onset of hypothermia you're suddenly in a windless, surprisingly sunny Spanish marina stripping off the layers and wondering what the fuss was all about. As Jimmy and Christian secured multiple lines and fenders to every external orifice they could find to stop the boat swinging around madly in the cross tide, I went to report in. Finally tracking down a helpful local lass who seemed surprised to see any sailors at all turn up in her little marina office, let alone a British one, I went through the traditional checking in procedures: passports; insurance and registration papers; etc, etc.

"How long you stay Ribadeo?" she asked.

"Good question", I responded unhelpfully but gave her a smile which probably didn't help but at least I tried.

Checking with 'the office' and talking to the owner we all agreed that I had failed in spectacular fashion to get the boat to Plymouth. We all agreed Ribadeo wasn't in Plymouth, in fact it wasn't even in the same country as Plymouth. I offered the observation I'd never been to Plymouth myself so could hardly tell but I guess that didn't help. The winter weather had shut the door in our faces and only a madman would keep going. Upon hearing that I was tempted of course, but 'the office' would have none of it. The weather would keep the boat in Ribadeo for weeks which meant it was time to go home since there was no rhyme or reason to charge the owner for 3 guys to sit in his boat when it wasn't going anywhere for a long time at least. We'd tried but we'd failed.

I wandered back to the boat. Jimmy and Christian had dutifully plugged us in to shore power and had filled the water tanks with fresh Spanish ria water. Now Jimmy stood on deck in his sea boots using the hose to wash away all the salty grime that had covered the vessel in our final valiant but doomed effort to get across Biscay. Christian was down below, cleaning the galley, probably with a toothbrush. I finished off the final log entry, recorded the total miles run and started packing away the salt stained slightly damp feeling charts. Of course, we use electronic charting software too, but I still get the old sheets out to give me, and the crew, the 'big picture' that you only really get with good old-fashioned charts. Perhaps I'm more salty than I thought?

Having made a decent start on cleaning and clearing the boat we made our way up the steeps steps into the town of Ribadeo itself perched above us. The sun had long since gone down and we stumbled around for a while trying to find a place to eat. Not much was open but eventually we found a hidden away local tapas bar and we ordered bread, chorizo, local tortilla, pimentos de padron (watch out for the hidden Jalapeño), calamari and washed it all down with a couple of jugs of Rioja.

We took a stroll after eating and found ourselves wandering higher into town until I spotted the local Parador, cool state run hotels that are rather posh and none too cheap too but they do tend to have great views from their balconies and patios and this one was no different. In expansive mood, Jimmy ordered a round of Spanish brandies. Jimmy likes brandy and, as an end of evening night cap you could do much worse, so we all demurred and grabbed seats outside. Wrapped in our jackets and sipping the warm brandy the coolness of the evening was all relative to the cold of actually being out at sea. Here looking east across the Galician ria, we could easily make out the twinkling lights of Castropol in the neighbouring province of Asturias. Beneath us, the red and green navigational lights in the channel steadfastly flashed away, happily unaware that there were no boats to guide to safety now. The ria was empty of shipping. Everyone had fled the sea and returned to the safety of the shore. Then a long sunken thought suddenly drifted up from the deep.

"Beerkeg?" I exclaimed.

Jimmy, lost in introspection himself, looked up suddenly.

"Beerkeg? What kind of name is that anyway? Where on Earth do the 'Beerkegs' come from?!"

Jimmy casually took a sip of brandy. He held the large glass in his enormous hands in proper brandy style, cupping the bowl in his palm and swilling it round gently, warming the nectar. Next to him, Christian, apparently lost in thought himself, seemed to be enjoying his own private reminiscences as he sat cosily nursing his drink, looking more childlike than normal, grinning away quietly whilst emitting occasional little chuckles. Although he was probably just drunk.

"An ancient race the Beerkegs", Jimmy declared. "Not many of them left now skipper... Where did the name come from? Well pretty obviously a Medieval landlord or innkeeper or some such. Lost in time I suppose...", he trailed off.

From the balcony of the Parador I looked to my left, northwards out to sea. In the dark and from our sheltered spot it seemed remarkably calm from here. Deceptively calm. Despite the tell-tale scudding clouds the moon was out, a gibbous moon which is the one everyone has forgotten about, and it shed its gentle illumination over the vast Cantabrian sea. Biscay, that ancient graveyard of ships, beckoned to us. But not this time. No. Not this time. Tomorrow we would fly back, tails between our legs, to wherever we came from. Back to the land for a while at least then regroup with more strangers and do the whole thing again on a different boat in different waters with new and exciting things breaking. And every voyage will be different and unique and unrepeatable. And always just a moment in time.

And that's the way it is I guess. Jimmy and I. Me and Jimmy. And the Sea of course. Always the Sea.

ACKNOWLEDGEMENT

To all those brave souls that have willingly boarded an unknown vessel, placed their trust in their Skipper, cast off the lines and ventured out into the big blue yonder. You know who you are.

In sympathy.